TRANSFORMING LITERACY TEACHING

IN THE ERA OF HIGHER STANDARDS

Model Lessons and Practical Strategies That Show You
How to Integrate the Standards to Plan and Teach With Confidence

Maria P. Walther

■ SCHOLASTIC

New York • Toronto • London • Auckland • Sydney
Mexico City • New Delhi • Hong Kong • Buenos Aires

DEDICATION

To my IPSD #204 ELA teammates: Melinda Lippe, Sandy Sobin, Becky Trybus, Hillary Lafferty, and Lynn Domck—who not only helped transform my thinking about literacy instruction in the Common Core era, but also stood up for what they believed was best for young learners.

ACKNOWLEDGMENTS

Many of the ideas in this book were sparked by the collaborative conversations I've had with my colleagues, and the energy to keep writing was fueled by the people in my life who are always there when I need them. Many thanks to . . .

- Katherine Phillips, my colleague, classroom neighbor, and dear friend. This year marks our 20th anniversary of teaching together. (Can you believe it?)

- My Graham School teammates, Kathy Williams and Kristin Creighton, who welcomed me with big smiles and a willingness to try new things, and my Brooks School teammates Sarah Cooley, Mary Ann Frantzen, and Margie Retzler, with whom I've shared a lot of laughs and a few tears.

- Karen Biggs-Tucker and Brian Tucker, who joined me on this writing adventure.

- All of my Judson MLIT students, whose passion for learning inspires me, and to Dr. Steven Layne, the program director, who nudges us out of our comfort zones.

- My fellow book fanatics at Anderson's Bookshop in Naperville, IL—year after year, you work to inspire readers and celebrate authors.

- The following publishers: Albert Whitman, Chronicle, Disney/Hyperion, HarperCollins, Lerner, and Macmillan Publishing Group; they help me stay on top of the latest and greatest literature for kids.

- My first graders at Graham and Brooks Elementary Schools whose questions, thoughts, and ideas teach me everything I need to know.

- Joanna Davis-Swing, my editor. Thanks for sticking with me on this one! It took longer than we expected, but I think the result was well worth the extra time.

- My husband of 25 years, Lenny, and our daughter, Katie, who is just starting her teaching career. You guys are the best!

Cover Designer: Jorge J. Namerow
Editor: Joanna Davis-Swing
Interior Designer: Sarah Morrow
Copyright © 2015 by Maria Walther
All rights reserved. Published by Scholastic Inc.
Printed in the U.S.A.
ISBN: 978-0-545-61400-9

1 2 3 4 5 6 7 8 9 10   40   22 21 20 19 18 17 16 15

Contents

A Call to Action

I'm excited to share my thinking about the new essentials for teaching young literacy learners in the era of higher standards. I view the implementation of higher standards as a call to action for primary-grade teachers. Teaching with the standards in mind offers us an opportunity to refocus our literacy instruction on the big picture—meaningful, connected, and in-depth learning for our students. The standards give us permission to discard the laundry list of separate skills and strategies that we've been handed by publishers or mandated by administrators who want us to deliver "the program" with fidelity—an approach which, as Richard Allington (2013) points out, ". . . is ironic because no research existed then, or exists now, to suggest maintaining fidelity to a core reading program will provide effective reading lessons" (p. 523). Letting the standards guide our way, we can transform our classrooms into inquiry-based learning communities where we learn alongside our students. Together, with our learners, we'll discover how readers, writers, listeners, and speakers think, make decisions, and communicate their ideas.

In this book, I'll answer the call to action and demonstrate how to plan literacy instruction with the big picture in mind. To help guide your transformation, the book is divided into two parts.

Part 1, entitled "The New Essentials of Literacy Teaching in the Era of Higher Standards," consists of four chapters. In Chapter 1, you will see how to plant seeds that will help learners form bonds and become a cohesive classroom community in which standards-based learning can flourish. In Chapter 2, I will further illuminate the notion of meaningful, in-depth, integrated literacy instruction. Then, in Chapters 3 and 4, I'll revisit and refine my earlier thinking about reading and writing workshops, building on the lessons and ideas in the books I wrote with my colleague, Katherine Phillips: *Month-by-Month Trait-Based Writing Instruction* (2009) and *Month-by-Month Reading Instruction for the Differentiated Classroom* (2012).

Part 2, entitled "Transforming Literacy Teaching Through Inquiry Experiences," includes three chapters in which I'll guide you in transforming teaching routines (Chapter 5) and planning and implementing inquiry experiences (Chapters 6 and 7). Chances are, some of these teaching routines, like read aloud and mini-lessons, are already part of your daily literacy instruction. My goal is to show you how to transform your current routines and create rich inquiry experiences. Luckily, this isn't hard to do. I've included many examples that illustrate possible teaching scenarios and how you can make minor teaching moves that will nudge your children toward reaching the complexity of thought and application of knowledge that the standards expect. As an added bonus, this type of planning will also save instructional time, something we all strive to do! Finally, in the online resources (see page 160), you will find planning guides to support you in the complex task of mapping out literacy instruction, along with video clips that show teaching ideas in action. On page 6, there is a chart that details how the ideas in this book will help you transform your literacy teaching.

You'll notice that I've used the Common Core State Standards (CCSS) as exemplar standards to guide our thinking. I realize that there is much debate across the nation about the standards and about the assessments that accompany them. Whether you are teaching in a state that has adopted the Common Core State Standards or one in which you are developing your own standards to reflect the rigor found in the CCSS, I think we can all agree that readjusting our expectations to ensure that learners are successful long after they leave our classrooms is a worthy goal and deserving of ongoing conversation.

TRANSFORMING TEACHING

I have too many separate skills and strategies to teach—where do I begin? How do I fit it all in across the school year?	In the pages that follow, I will show you how to integrate learning experiences to help children understand the connections among foundational skills, language skills, reading, writing, thinking, listening, and speaking. In addition, in the online resources (see page 160) you'll find guides to assist you as you plan.
I'm always running out of time and feeling rushed during my reading and writing workshops. How do I make more time for my learners to read, converse, and write?	As you read this book, you'll learn how to save time and teach with more depth by selecting standards-focused learning target or "big ideas" to explore in both reading and writing workshop at the same time, or during a combined literacy workshop.
I teach primary-grade learners, and they are always following me around asking what to do next! How do I nudge them toward independence?	When you release responsibility to your students by putting them in charge of their learning, you'll find their independence grows. That's what Chapter 1 is all about!
I'm looking for the best books to read aloud to my students to spark collaborative conversations about texts, to serve as mentor texts for writing, and to assist me in teaching the concepts found in the language standards. Do you know any good titles?	Fortunately, you are reading a professional book written by a children's literature fanatic. Most of the inquiry experiences include a book suggestion or two!

Transforming Teaching

You'll notice Transforming Teaching charts just like the one above throughout this book. Why? Because in our evolution as literacy teachers we are continually examining our current practice to reflect on how our teaching choices impact student learning. Then, we synthesize new learning from professional development experiences along with the growing knowledge of our students to refine our craft or take it to the next step. So, whether you are using the Common Core State Standards or not, my hope is that this book helps you examine your practice, then nudges you to ponder and converse with colleagues to determine how you can transform your teaching and students' learning experiences. Let's begin our work together as we transform our teaching!

Chapter 1

Planting the Seeds

A Packet of Seeds

One of the most beloved titles in the stacks of children's books that crowd my office is *Mrs. Spitzer's Garden* by Edith Pattou. I often share this book with teachers when I'm speaking to them at the beginning of the year. Edith Pattou's book, dedicated to a kindergarten teacher, reminds us of the awesome responsibility that we have as primary-grade teachers. At the beginning of each year, when our principal hands us the diverse "packet of seeds," we are, in fact, planting a wildflower garden that we will carefully tend all year long (even through the long winter months!). What we must keep in mind is that much of the work we do as primary teachers is like watering, weeding, and spreading sunshine on a garden. Often, we don't get to admire the colorful blooms of this daily work, but Pattou pens it perfectly when she says, "But the plants will keep growing, uncurling their stems, stretching their leaves outward, and showing their faces to the sun" (2001, unpaged). So, with Pattou's metaphor in our minds, we begin our journey together by sowing the seeds for yearlong learning.

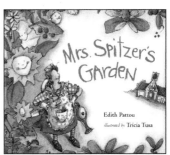

Go online to view a video classroom tour of my classroom; see page 160.

A Yearlong Journey

For many of us, a major shift is that the Common Core State Standards are end-of-the-year expectations. The standards specify the end destination of a yearlong journey. That journey will vary based on the needs of your students. How, then, do we effectively implement the standards for the youngest learners? We begin by asking the big picture question—what is it we want our students to know and be able to do when they walk out of our classrooms at the end of a school year? Luckily for us, the answer to this "big picture" question appears in the standards document.

Create an environment where children become self-directed, independent learners.

A Portrait of a Learner Who Meets Rigorous Standards

❊ Becomes a self-directed, independent learner

❊ Builds strong content-area knowledge

❊ Adjusts communication based on audience, task, purpose, and content

❊ Comprehends as well as critiques

❊ Seeks to understand other perspectives and cultures

❊ Evaluates other points of view critically and constructively

❊ Values evidence

❊ Uses technology and digital media strategically and capably

Common Core State Standards (CCSS) for English Language Arts *(NGA Center/CCSSO, 2010, p. 7)*

I've summarized their expectations in the box on this page, painting a portrait of a learner who meets standards. In the pages that follow, I'll share how to begin the journey by creating the type of learning environment that fosters each of the characteristics so that by year's end, your children will embody the type of student who, like the students in Mrs. Spitzer's class, will continue to grow and learn long after he or she leaves our classroom.

Create a Classroom Environment That Encourages Self-Directed, Independent Learning

We've all heard the adage, "Actions speak louder than words." I'd like to revise the adage a bit: "Actions, reactions, and being proactive, along with our words, speak volumes about what we believe." Let me explain what I mean by this and how it helps shape not only my classroom environment, but also students' view of themselves long after they leave my room. I'll begin with actions and reactions.

CONSIDER ACTIONS AND REACTIONS

You know that students hang on your every word. You see them "pretending" they are you by mimicking the way you read aloud (apparently I always cross my legs) and the way you act and talk. They even imitate the way you hold a pencil. I've noticed that it is tricky for first graders to tuck a pencil behind their tiny ears, but they still try! If you've ever invited someone to videotape you while you're teaching, you've probably observed your own unconscious actions and language patterns, especially if you've been teaching for a long time, like I have. In fact, when I read Peter Johnston's book *Choice Words* (2004) for the first time, I found that I had phrases in my teaching vocabulary that I needed to "unlearn." In this section,

Transforming Literacy Teaching in the Era of Higher Standards, K–2 © 2015 by Maria P. Walther, Scholastic Teaching Resources

I've summarized the wisdom I've gained from reading and listening to well-known literacy mentors like Peter Johnston, Debbie Miller, and Ellin Keene. Their work has helped me transform my teaching by focusing on my language, actions, and reactions. If you haven't already, I would encourage you to read their books listed in the box below to deepen your understanding of the ideas I've touched on here.

Show children what it means to be respectful, caring, and kind. Pause and take advantage of teachable moments by pointing out students who display these character traits. Take the time to say, "Wow! Joseph, thanks for helping Anisha pick up her pencil box when it fell. That's what friends do!" Model expected respectful behaviors. For example, during whole-class discussions when Sami is sharing her thinking, I now request that the rest of the class put their hands down. That way we can all focus on Sami's ideas. This also shows Sami (and the other students) that I'm going to give her time to think and share *before* moving on to the next student. Then, when she's done I might say, "Who would like to add to Sami's ideas? Who has different thinking to share?" I realize that these encounters take a few extra minutes, but every moment spent noticing and modeling expected behaviors will pay off. I promise!

Show children what it means to be a respectful listener.

Use language that promotes agency. Debbie Miller (*Reading With Meaning*, 2013b) and Peter Johnston (*Choice Words*, 2004) have taught me to use language that encourages students to believe that "I'm the kind of kid who can figure this out." I strive to do this in my classroom. So when children come to me with a problem I might say, "How do you think you might solve that problem?" Once the child has developed a strategy, I send him or her off to try it and to let me know how it goes. Later, I follow up by providing time for that student to share his or her smart solution with the class so that we can all learn from it.

Think about how you respond to students' thoughts and actions. When responding to your students' thinking, try to remove judgment from your words. So instead of saying "good idea," you might simply say "Hmmmm!" as you consider that thought, or respond with "thank you." For more phrases to help you respond to students' thinking see the box on page 10. Many teachers, myself included, have used the phrase, "I like the way you . . ." This phrase "offers a judgment and implies that the point of a child's efforts is to please you" (Johnston, 2012, p. 42). Instead, consider making a conscious effort to transform your response language to alternatives such as:

Professional Books About Using Language to Mediate Learning Experiences

❋ *Choice Words: How Our Language Affects Children's Learning* (Johnston, 2004)

❋ *Opening Minds: Using Language to Change Lives* (Johnston, 2012)

❋ *Reading With Meaning: Teaching Comprehension in the Primary Grades* (Miller, 2013b)

❋ *Talk About Understanding: Rethinking Classroom Talk to Enhance Comprehension* (Keene, 2012)

- Look at how you . . .

- Because you added those details to your picture, the reader can better understand your message.

- When you listened carefully to what your friend was saying, you got even smarter.

- You found a good way to do that. Can you think of other ways that would also work?

The Language of Responding to Students' Thinking

❋ Interesting! Hmmmm! Wow!

❋ Let's see if I've got this right.

❋ Can anyone add to his or her thinking?

❋ Would you agree with that? Why/why not?

❋ Do you have the same thinking, or is your thinking different? Why?

❋ Can you say more about that?

❋ Thanks for straightening me out!

❋ Wow! I never thought about it like that before!

❋ How did you know that?

❋ Are there any other ways to think about that?

(Johnston, 2004) (Walther & Phillips, 2012)

Give process-oriented feedback. When we respond to students' successes with phrases that focus on effort such as, "You tried really hard" or those that highlight effective strategy use like "You found a smart way to solve that problem. Can you think of another way?" we are giving feedback on the process. Process-oriented feedback helps learners independently solve problems the next time they are faced with a similar situation. Keep in mind that "the purpose of feedback is to improve conceptual understanding or increase strategic options while developing stamina, resilience, and motivation—expanding the vision of what is possible and how to get there. Perhaps we could call it *feedforward* rather than feedback" (Johnston, 2012, p. 48).

Like any habit, changing your actions and reactions will take time and practice. Don't be afraid to post a few key phrases in a place where you can see them. That's what I do. Along with your "in the moment" actions and reactions, being proactive by thoughtfully planning the physical arrangement of your teaching space further creates a community where independence can flourish.

BE PROACTIVE

To create a classroom environment where children are empowered to grow as self-directed, independent learners, it is helpful if we know our end goals and structure our physical classroom environment and learning experiences to meet these goals. In the past three years, I have had the opportunity to pack, unpack, and set up my entire classroom twice. This experience has given me unique insights into the importance of the physical classroom setup. I love figuring out how to create purposeful spaces where students can comfortably read, work, and learn together. In the online resources (see page 160), you'll find a video clip that features a tour of my classroom. The following are a few additional tips to get you started in creating a purposeful physical classroom setup:

- Consider using some tables instead of all desks.

- Design a space for collaborative conversations with enough room for your class to sit in a circle.

- Create an area to gather for read-alouds and other whole-class experiences (usually the same area as above).

- Maintain a well-stocked classroom library that changes throughout the year.

- Place books around the room so that the first items children or adults see when they walk into your room is BOOKS!

Transforming Literacy Teaching in the Era of Higher Standards, K–2 © 2015 by Maria P. Walther, Scholastic Teaching Resources

- Arrange spots where students can work together with partners or in small groups and where you can confer and meet with small groups.

- Leave the walls blank at the beginning of the year so that you can fill them with anchor charts and other evidence of students' thinking and work.

- Take and display photos of your busy learners working.

- Add personal touches such as pillows (with removable covers), lamps, plants, and other items that make you and your students feel welcome and at home.

Purposeful classroom design plays an important role in making children feel comfortable and in control of their own learning. As you introduce the different areas in your classroom to your students, it is essential that you collaborate to develop guidelines for accessing and learning together in these spaces. Shared guidelines recorded on anchor charts like the one below are helpful and provide students with clear expectations that you can revisit, when needed, throughout the year. After all, to add my own spin on the repeated line found in Daniel's Pinkwater's book *The Big Orange Splot* (1977), you want your students to feel about your classroom they way Mr. Plumbean felt about his house: "Our classroom is us and we are it. Our classroom is where we want to be and looks like all of our dreams."

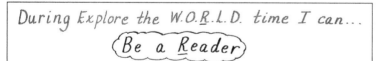

During *Explore the W.O.R.L.D.* time I can...

(Be a **R**eader)

READERS are...
* Finding a good reading spot (1 pillow, please)
* Reading the whole time
* Reading on their own or with a friend
* Taking turns with the books
* Using a whisper voice
* Recommending books to a friend
* Taking care of the books
* Putting books back in their place

Readers are learning...
* How to be an even better reader
* What kinds of books they like to read
* Facts from nonfiction books
* Ideas for their own writing
* That we read to learn (Graham)
* That we read to get smart (Peyton)

Collaborate to develop guidelines for learning together in the classroom.

Consider using some tables instead of all desks.

Arrange spots for students to work together with partners or in small groups.

Add personal touches such as pillows.

Weave Content-Area Learning Experiences Throughout the Day

If our goal as primary teachers is to help students build strong content-area knowledge, then we need to rethink relegating content-area studies to the last half hour of our day. Instead, look for ways to weave content-rich learning throughout the day. The simplest way to meet this goal is by selecting read-aloud texts to enhance learning experiences or match the interests of your learners. For example, when Darius got a new pet lizard, we celebrated by reading *Lizards* (Bishop, 2010). When the first snowflakes are falling outside, I always share *Snow Is Falling* (Branley, 1986/2000).

When I'm guiding readers in small groups, my students independently apply their learning during what Katherine Phillips and I have dubbed Explore the W. O. R. L. D. (Walther & Phillips, 2012). During Explore the W. O. R. L. D. time, students have the opportunity to be Writers, Observers, Readers, Listeners, and Word Detectives. The "Be an Observer" center was created so that we could infuse content-area learning into students' daily literacy routines and provide time for students to read, observe, discuss, and explore content-related books and materials. Observers are always excited to share their new learning, and I'm amazed at how much they discover on their own when they are given time to observe, think, and learn together. In this area, or in a basket, I place books and materials that match our science or social studies topics. Students can record their observations on individual recording sheets or in a "Be an Observer" notebook found in the online resources (see page 160) that they use only in this center. You could also have them record their observations on sticky notes and add them to a nearby chart entitled "What I Noticed/What I Learned." Later, during sharing time, children can share what they've learned from their research with the rest of the class.

Another strategy is posting a content-related Question of the Week. The first time you do this, demonstrate how researchers might go about answering a question. Show children how to use multiple sources by locating reliable information via online sources, searching for the answer in an informational book by accessing the table of contents or index, asking an expert, and so on. Provide a place for students to post their answers along with their sources. The following are a few sample questions:

- Who is on the penny? What can you teach us about that person?
- Why are the days getting shorter? Why is it getting darker earlier?
- How do different kinds of beetles protect themselves from predators?
- Why do plants have leaves?
- Why do turtles have shells?

Strategies for Weaving Content-Area Learning Throughout the Day

❋ Read aloud content-rich texts.

❋ Create a content-based center or work station.

❋ Post a question of the week.

❋ Pause to read and learn from bulletin boards.

❋ Share current events.

Infuse content-area learning into students' daily literacy routines.

Next time you walk your students to or from lunch, notice the bulletin boards on the way. Often your colleagues and their students have posted a synopsis of their learning about a content area. Stop, invite children to sit in front of the bulletin board and learn together. To follow up this experience, write a thank-you note to the other class informing them about what you learned.

Create a space in your room where you and your students can post age-appropriate current events. At the primary grade level, you might label this space something like, "What's Happening at Brooks School, in Aurora, and in Our World." Here you can post school events, events at the library or in town, or world events that relate to content you are studying such as space travel, the biggest pumpkin grown, and so on. The content-area ideas I've discussed here are summarized in the box on page 12.

Along with the Standards for English Language Arts explored in this book, the Common Core Math Standards and Next Generation Science Standards provide clear content expectations. Although I will not be addressing the specifics of the standards for math and science, wise teachers like you know that it is essential to help young learners see the interconnectedness of all of their learning. In Chapter 2, I will fully explore the similarities between the English Language Arts, Math, and Science practices to help you make these shared habits of mind a part of your classroom instruction every day.

Encourage Communication About a Variety of Topics for Various Audiences, Tasks, and Purposes

One of the features of this book is a collection of teaching routines (see Chapter 5) and inquiry experiences (Chapters 6 and 7). The ongoing routines and experiences are designed to provide your students with rich opportunities to communicate purposefully in a variety of ways. To enhance the learning, think about calling attention to some of the routines you already have in place. Discuss and record the audience, task, and purpose so that your learners begin to understand how and why their communication varies.

We Communicate for Different Reasons

Audience (Who?)	Task (What?)	Purpose (Why?)
Peers	Talking with my classmates	To understand the thinking of others
Upper-grade book buddies	Listening to a read-aloud	To listen to an expert read
The school community	Creating bulletin boards	To share our learning
My teacher	Conferring with my teacher	To think and talk about my reading or writing
Me	Reading independently	To get to be an even better reader

I think that sometimes we assume that our learners understand the "who, what, and why" of our everyday practices. By creating an anchor chart like the one pictured above, you can clearly call attention to the audience, task, and purpose of your daily routines. Adding to this chart throughout the year will build on this understanding as you introduce other learning experiences.

Now, you've gathered a few tips on creating a community of self-directed students who learn about content and communication throughout their day. Next, we turn to supporting children as they learn with and from each other.

Help Young Learners Understand, Accept, and Celebrate the Perspectives and Cultures of Others

Although the next three characteristics of college- and career-ready learners are separated for organizational purposes, you'll notice that they are closely linked and interdependent. Learners who seek to understand the cultures and perspectives of others will be better equipped to evaluate their peers' points of view critically and constructively so that they can not only comprehend but also critique the message. To begin, let's look at how to set up an environment and learning experiences that will help young children begin to understand the cultures and perspectives of others. The key word in the previous sentence is "understand." What leads to true understanding? Again, I turn to some of the thinkers who have helped me to grasp this concept. In their book *The Understanding By Design Guide to Creating High-Quality Units*, Grant Wiggins and Jay McTighe (2011) tell us that the "ultimate test of genuine understanding concerns the ability to transfer: What can learners do with what they have learned in school?" (p. 92). Ellin Keene elaborates, "When we understand deeply, we experience words and ideas that we find beautiful or compelling; we change our thinking, often reexamining our values and beliefs; we actually generate new thinking and ideas; we are occasionally inspired; and we remember and reuse what we have learned" (2012, p. 20).

In both of these professional books, the authors identify empathy as an indicator of deep comprehension and understanding. Empathy is an individual's ability to walk in another's shoes and uncover potential value in what others might find odd, unfamiliar, or improbable. In the primary-grade classroom, one way to enhance a child's ability to understand the diverse cultures and perspectives of others is to foster empathy through text-related experiences. A few questions you might ask to develop or assess empathy include the following:

- What would it be like to walk in [the character's] shoes?

- How might [the character] feel about [the event/experience/adventure]?

- What was [the author] trying to make us see or feel? (Wiggins & McTighe)

Help young learners understand the cultures of others.

As a reader, we experience empathy in literary texts when we are transported to the world of the book. Empathic readers become friends with the characters—experiencing the same feelings adventures, conflicts, and challenges (Keene, 2012). In his book *Opening Minds* (2012), Peter Johnston takes the notion of empathy a step further when he stresses the importance of helping children develop their "social imagination" or their ability to figure out the "social-emotional logic that lies behind behavior" (p. 69). Both Ellin Keene and Peter Johnston say that a good place to start with developing empathy and social imagination is by having collaborative conversations about

Transforming Literacy Teaching in the Era of Higher Standards, K–2 © 2015 by Maria P. Walther, Scholastic Teaching Resources

books that have emotional tensions and conflicts. I've included a few of my favorite books in the chart below. When conversing about such books, spark conversations with the ideas that follow:

- Can you tell by the look on my face how I'm feeling about what just happened in the book?
- How do you think [the character] is feeling right now? How can you tell?
- How do you think [the character] feels about that?
- [The character] is worried/sad/scared/happy. Can you show me what a worried/sad/scared/happy face might look like?
- Imagine what it might feel like to be [the character] right now.
- Why do you think [the author] made [the character] say that?

A Few of My Favorite Books for
Developing Empathy and Social Imagination

Bully (Seeger, 2013)	When gray bull tells brown bull to go away, brown bull's feelings are hurt. His hurt turns into anger, and he begins to bully his animal friends, growing larger with each insult. Then, goat calls him a bully and he rethinks his actions.
Each Kindness (Woodson, 2012)	Chloe learns a life lesson when her teacher points out the power of kindness. After this compelling lesson, Chloe wishes she had shown kindness to the new girl, Maya, instead ignoring of her because she was less fortunate and different. Unfortunately, Chloe never gets the chance to show kindness because Maya moves away.
Pug & Doug (Breen, 2013)	Even friends who both love listening to polka music and have a secret "pawshake" can have their own unique interests. When a misunderstanding threatens their friendship, Pug and Doug agree to, "...talk things over. Because that's what best friends do."
The Story of Fish and Snail (Freeman, 2013)	Fish craves adventure and seeks out books with pirates and treasure. Snail prefers books with princesses or kittens and is content to wait for Fish to come back and tell a story. When Fish leaves without Snail to find another book, Snail follows and, together, the two friends embark on an adventure.

Children who can walk in another's shoes and understand the feelings and motivations behind another's actions and reactions are on the road to being able to look at a situation from different points of view and, eventually, evaluate those points of view.

Introduce the Concept of Point of View

In order to help students evaluate the points of view of others critically and constructively, we must first introduce the concept of point of view to our "me-centered" learners. The foundation of that introduction is our work with empathy—inviting learners to walk in someone else's shoes. Now, adding to students' ability to empathize, we introduce another facet of understanding identified by Wiggins and McTighe (2011)—*perspective*. Young children who demonstrate perspective can begin to see the big picture. We start to build their awareness that other people may have a different point of view than their own. Eventually, we enable them to take a critical or disinterested stance and recognize and avoid bias in how positions are stated. When discussing texts or topics with multiple viewpoints, you can ask questions similar to those that follow to nudge children toward seeing the bigger picture.

- What are the different points of view or ways to think about [a particular topic or occurrence in a text or in real life]?

- How might this look from [a character's or classmate's] perspective?

- How is [the character's or classmate's] thinking similar to/different from [another character's or classmate's] thinking?

- What are other possible reactions to [an occurrence in a text or in real life]?

You will find an inquiry experience and book titles to broaden students' understanding of point of view on pages 124–125. By guiding our learners as they empathize with characters and classmates and begin to consider the fact that there is more than one "right" answer, approach, or idea, we move them closer to being able to critique their own ideas and the ideas of others.

Develop Open-Mindedness to Help Students Critique as Well as Comprehend

At the International Reading Association Convention in 2012, I saw Roger Farr speak, and he said something that has stuck with me ever since: "Reading is thought guided by written symbols." For our youngest readers, it is important that we develop and enhance their thought processes while at the same time guiding them to better understand the written symbols. In fact, over the years I've noticed that some of my best thinkers are not necessarily my best readers, yet. One way to enhance your students' thought process is by opening their minds to the views of others, as well as by developing an environment where children feel comfortable when their peers disagree with or critique their ideas. We've already put the following "markers" in place in our classrooms:

- Awareness and acceptance of differences in each other, in activities, and in thinking perspectives

- Understanding of classmates and their diverse perspectives

- Ability to listen carefully to the thinking of others and consider their points of view on a given topic

How do we, as teachers, help our students open their minds to the fact that learning is an ongoing process that evolves and can be enhanced by listening to the thoughtful critiques of others? On the flipside, how do we teach our students to critique each other's ideas in a helpful and respectful manner? As always, we lead by example. Along with the strategies found in the box on page 17, when we share an idea, we might open the conversation with statements such as the following:

 Transforming Literacy Teaching in the Era of Higher Standards, K–2 © 2015 by Maria P. Walther, Scholastic Teaching Resources

- Do you agree or disagree with that idea?
- Tell us what you're thinking about that idea.
- Do you have another perspective for us to consider?

Day by day, conversation after conversation, we show children the value of incorporating the ideas of others into their own thinking. When learners share their ideas or critique the ideas of others, it is important that they begin to understand the value of evidence-based conversations, writing, and speaking.

Value Evidence

The standards are asking us to raise a generation of educated, critical citizens who are able to listen to or read a claim and ask the following questions (Calkins, Ehrenworth, & Lehman, 2012, p. 10):

- "Who is making this claim?"
- "What is the person's evidence?"
- "What are the other positions?"
- "How can I compare and contrast these different views, think about the biases and assumptions behind them, weigh their warrants, and come to an evidence-based, well-reasoned stance?"

Strategies to Cultivate Open-Minded Conversations

- ❋ Launch conversations with open-ended questions like, "So, why do you think . . ."
- ❋ Provide ample wait time.
- ❋ Refrain from judging students' responses; instead ask, "What do the rest of you think?"
- ❋ Take students ideas seriously.
- ❋ Begin your ideas with words like, "Perhaps," "Maybe," or "I'm wondering . . ."

(Johnston, 2012)

Everything that we've discussed thus far in this chapter will lead children to become educated, critical citizens. Our greatest challenge as primary teachers is distilling the "big ideas" contained in the standards into reasonable, developmentally appropriate concepts for children ages five to eight. What does a conversation about evidence sound like in a primary-grade classroom? I believe, and the standards echo this belief, that we begin by showing children how to find evidence for their ideas in the illustrations and words in picture books and other texts and then build from there. In the box on page 19, I'll share an evidence-based, read-aloud experience for kindergartners using the familiar book *The Very Hungry Caterpillar* by Eric Carle (1969/1987). Later, in Part 2, you'll find other teaching routines and inquiry experiences that help children become critical readers and listeners.

In addition to helping students focus on evidence, it is critical that we, as teachers, continually work to become educated, critical professionals who are able to provide a research-based rationale for our practices to parents, administrators, and other stakeholders. More important, as we transform our teaching to meet higher standards, it is essential that we don't abandon evidence-based practices in our classrooms. To grow as professionals, it is important that we make deliberate choices about our ongoing learning. Our actions, both in and outside our classroom, impact our learners. You, too, have to value the evidence that you discover by being part of a professional learning community. On page 18 you will find "A Portrait of an Accomplished Teacher." Notice how it mirrors "A Portrait of a Learner Who Meets Rigorous Standards" on which this chapter was based. As we transform our teaching practices, it makes sense that our behaviors should reflect those we expect from our young learners. To reach these goals, I've provided a few helpful tips for keeping current with evidence-based practices in the box on page 18.

A Portrait of an Accomplished Teacher

❋ Independently seeks out self-directed professional learning experiences

❋ Actively participates in professional learning communities

❋ Builds strong content-area knowledge

❋ Adjusts instruction based on students' interests and learning needs

❋ Analyzes as well as critiques his own teaching practices

❋ Values evidence and uses data to make instructional decisions

❋ Seeks to understand the perspectives and cultures of her students, her students' families, and her colleagues

❋ Evaluates other points of view critically and constructively

❋ Uses technology and digital media strategically and capably

I realize that the concepts of empathy, social imagination, perspective, point of view, and the ability to evaluate and value evidence are complex concepts for our little learners. But trust me when I tell you that it is possible to design learning experiences to cultivate these cognitive outcomes one step at a time. As we continue on this journey together, I'll show you how. Next, we'll take a quick look at the role technology plays in the development of a learner.

Use Technology to Enhance Student Learning

Depending on when you were born and how much time you spend interacting with technology, you are either a digital native or digital immigrant. I, myself, am a digital immigrant. Even though I was on the cutting edge and purchased my first computer (an Apple II GS) in 1986 when I landed my first teaching job, I still feel like I'm always playing catch-up. Depending on the digital resources

Keeping Current With Evidence-Based Practices

❋ Be an active reader, writer, and thinker.

❋ Keep a reader's and a writer's notebook. Share with students what you are reading, writing, and thinking about. It is so important for them to see you living a reader's and a writer's life, too!

❋ Start a teacher's notebook. Purchase a small notebook to record your notes from professional development experiences, your thinking and reflections, or new book titles you discover. You can organize it by adding sticky tabs labeled with the following categories: *Observations, Discussions/Charts, Books, Things to Do, Notes From Professional Development Sessions, Other* (Walther & Phillips, 2012, p. 8).

❋ Engage in book discussions with your colleagues of both professional books and books you have read for pleasure!

❋ Find colleagues with similar philosophies. Meet, talk, share, reflect, argue, debate and learn together!

❋ Join Twitter, follow blogs, or access other social media resources where you can network with teachers who share the same passions about education that you do.

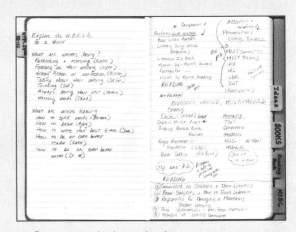

Create a teacher's notebook.

An Evidence-Based Conversation in Kindergarten

If you were going to carry on an evidence-based conversation using the book *The Very Hungry Caterpillar* (Carle, 1969/1987), it might sound something like this:

BEFORE READING

❄ Set the purpose for reading and share the learning target by saying, "The title of this book is *The Very Hungry Caterpillar*. Let's read to find out why Eric Carle chose to give this book that title. Let's see if we can find any evidence in his illustrations or words that the caterpillar is 'very hungry.' Evidence is when you find proof or a reason to believe that something is true. Are you ready to be a reading detective and see if you can spot some evidence or proof?"

DURING READING

❄ One Sunday . . . page: Ask, "Did you hear any evidence on this page? Was the evidence in the pictures or words? [words] Is that enough proof to make you believe the caterpillar is very hungry or do you need more evidence?"

❄ Continue that conversation as you read the Monday–Friday pages.

❄ On Saturday . . . page [where the caterpillar eats ALL the different foods]: Ask, "Hmmmm! What are you thinking now?"

❄ Guide students to see that this page is full of text and illustration-based evidence by posing the following questions/prompts:

- "How did you figure that out?"

- "Show us where you saw that in the illustrations."

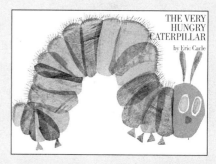

AFTER READING

Wrap up the experience with, "Now that you've had time to search for evidence, do you think *The Very Hungry Caterpillar* is a good title for this book? Why or why not? How did looking for evidence help you as a reader?"

that are available in your classroom and school, and the amount of professional development you've had related to those resources, it can be an ongoing challenge to meaningfully integrate technology into the curriculum for young learners. I am fortunate to have colleagues who have nudged me in the right direction, but I am still developing my expertise as I strive to seamlessly integrate technology and interactive media throughout the day. In this book, I'll share what I've learned so far!

As a teacher of early learners, an organization I often turn to for advice on developmentally appropriate practices is the National Association for the Education of Young Children (NAEYC). NAEYC and the Fred Rogers Center for Early Learning and Children's Media (2012) created a position statement that provides the following useful guidelines for using technology and interactive media to enhance learning for young children:

- View selecting appropriate technology as you would making decisions about any instructional material you might use in your classroom—exercise your professional judgment to make reflective, responsive, and intentional choices that will promote positive outcomes for each child.

- Harness the power of technology to help children effectively communicate their ideas and feelings, investigate the environment, and locate evidence or information.

- Use technological tools to build relationships, maintain ongoing communication, exchange information, and share online resources with students' families.

Technology and interactive media are an embedded aspect of students' lives. Oftentimes, our young learners know as much as we do, or more, about the technological tools in our classrooms. Our overarching goal is to view technology as we would any other learning tool and discover ways to integrate it throughout the day in authentic ways in order to enhance and extend student learning. Seamless integration takes place when the use of technology and media becomes routine and transparent—when the child's (or teacher's) focus is on the activity or exploration itself and not on the technology or media being used (NAEYC, 2012). As you reflect on your own practice, think about how you are already using technology. Use the guidelines in the box at left to assess your current uses of technology and set goals for future uses. After all, reflection and self-assessment are two tools that we use as educators to transform our teaching and move forward. Let's return to the garden that we planted at the beginning of this chapter to find out what needs to be completed next.

Characteristics of Effective Uses of Technology

❄ Fosters active, hands-on, engaging, and empowering learning

❄ Gives children control

❄ Provides adaptive scaffolds to ease the accomplishment of tasks

❄ Helps children create, problem solve, consider, think, listen, view critically, make decisions, observe, document, research, investigate ideas, demonstrate learning, take turns, and learn with and from one another

❄ Is used as one of many options to support children's learning

(NAEYC, 2012, pp. 6–7)

A Garden Begins to Grow

Whether you are reading this book in the summer, fall, winter, or spring, there is always something you can be doing in your garden. You can choose to make small changes that will impact your learners tomorrow. In fact, I'm an advocate of "dabbling" with new ideas, routines, or structures at the end of the school year when I know my students well. Then, I can work out some of the kinks so that when the new year begins, I have a little practice under my belt. Whether this means relearning some phrases you commonly use, moving a bookshelf or desk, or committing to trying out one of the content-area ideas, it is never too late to start! It might mean pulling out a few weeds (abandoning practices that don't meet the standards), relocating a plant or two (switching your schedule to make more time to converse), or consulting with a fellow gardener (the best way to make changes!), but it is well worth the effort. What will you do tomorrow to ensure your plants continue to grow long after they leave your care?

Chapter 2

Discovering Connections

Less Is More

If you'd joined one of our "Tuesday Night Team" planning meetings a few years ago, you might have overheard comments like these: *I wish I had more time to spend on [a given topic]. I feel like I'm rushing through my day. I'm just skimming the surface, and some of my students are getting left behind.* In our professional learning community, my colleagues and I have been struggling with this dilemma for years. A decade before the higher standards arrived, we committed to a "less is more" mentality, supporting each other as we eliminated the "cute" activities from our teaching day, and it has made a big difference. But even after years zeroing in on the essentials, we still were mandated to teach too much material. Does this sound familiar? Enter the Common Core State Standards. Finally, a "less is more" document containing ten standards for reading, ten for writing, and six for speaking and listening. (Yes, I realize there are also foundational and language standards, but it is still much less than the nearly 100 English Language Arts Performance Descriptors we previously had in Illinois.) Better yet, the new standards are clearly integrated. Great! This was the answer we had been looking for! The structure and design of the standards compel us to focus on key concepts and essential questions.

Go online to view a video on Standards Integration in Action; see page 160.

Focus on Key Concepts and Essential Questions

Our questions about SPACE...

How did the planets get their names?

How do the planets get their colors?

Is there life on other planets?

How many planets are in our Solar System?

How many stars are in our Solar System?

Is there garbage in space?

How did Earth form?

How did the planets form?

What is Jupiter's red spot made of?

Why are there rings around Saturn?

Why isn't Pluto a planet anymore?

Why does Jupiter have a lot of storms?

What does an astronaut's space suit do?

What would it feel like to be on the moon?

How many astronauts have gone to space?

Who was the 1st astronaut to go to the moon?

Why do astronauts go to the moon?

Invite students to pose their own questions about a science-related topic.

Key Concepts for K–2 Learners

❋ Read to understand.

❋ Write to understand and communicate.

❋ Converse to understand and communicate.

❋ Ask and answer clarifying questions.

❋ Attend to key details.

❋ Ponder themes, central messages, and morals.

❋ Consider different points of view.

❋ Think about the author's, writer's, or speaker's purpose.

❋ Notice and apply different approaches to crafting text.

❋ Compare and contrast to better understand.

❋ Evaluate the message.

❋ Apply new learning to various contexts.

The interrelated nature of the standards helps streamline instruction because you can focus on one key concept applied to different learning contexts. For example, when planning experiences for students to ask and answer questions about key details, you might demonstrate how proficient readers ask questions while reading a story aloud. Then, during writing workshop, provide an opportunity for students to do the same as they listen to stories their peers have written. Next, you could invite students to pose their own questions about a science-related topic. I could go on, but I think you get the point. Focusing on key concepts embedded in the K–2 standards will bring depth to your students' learning and provide ample time to guide children to true understanding across instructional contexts. The best way to get started on your journey toward teaching for understanding is to look at the connections among the standards for reading, writing, speaking, and listening.

To help you clearly see the connections among the standards, I've organized the K–2 essential standards-related questions in the chart on page 23 to refer to as you plan your instruction. If you're not familiar with essential questions, let me share a little bit about them. The goal of an essential question is to help the learner "achieve greater focus, understanding, and efficacy when dealing with new challenges" (Wiggins & McTighe, 2011, p. 15). To elaborate, learning that is guided by essential questions engages students in active, inquiry-based experiences where they dig deep to look for familiar patterns, make connections, and figure

What Is Poetry?

A poet writes a poem.

Some poems rhyme.

Some poems have big and bold words

Some poems have repeated words.

Some poems have rhythm. (a steady beat)

Poets use conventions carefully. (punctuation)

Pose questions about key concepts.

Transforming Literacy Teaching in the Era of Higher Standards, K–2 © 2015 by Maria P. Walther, Scholastic Teaching Resources

out the best strategies to solve problems so that they can transfer their learning to new situations. Students often ask essential questions, or as I sometimes call them, "big questions," without our prompting—queries like *Why? How? What does it mean? Why is that important? What comes next?* Questions like these lead to meaning-making, which is important because "the point of school is not merely to know things but to become better at and more assertive about inquiry" (Wiggins & McTighe, 2011, p. 15). Notice when you look across each row of essential questions on the chart that the standards are clearly linked and centered on the key concepts found in the box on page 22.

Consider posting these key concepts somewhere in your classroom or in your lesson plan book. Refer to the concepts as you evaluate your instructional practices. Reflect by asking yourself, "Does this literacy lesson, activity, or routine lead students toward understanding and applying the concepts?" If not, it might be time to either abandon the activity or transform that particular instructional approach by taking it to the next step. Along with discovering the connections among the key ideas contained in the standards, it is also helpful to consider the connection between the hallmarks of proficient readers or listeners and proficient writers or speakers.

K–2 Essential Standards-Related Questions

Reading	Writing	Speaking/Listening
• How does reading every day help me as a learner?	• How does writing every day help me as a learner?	• How does having collaborative conversations every day help me as a learner?
• What is the author trying to say or teach me? How do I know?	• What am I trying to say or teach my readers? How will my readers know?	• What is the speaker trying to say or teach me? How do I know?
• What is the big idea/main topic of the text? How do I know?	• What is the big idea of my story? • What is the main topic of my informational text? • What is my opinion? • How will my readers know?	• What is the big idea/main topic that the speaker is trying to communicate? How do I know?
• How does thinking about the elements of stories help me better understand the meaning?	• What elements and details should I include in my stories?	• What key details or facts is the speaker trying to communicate? How do I know?
• How does thinking about the connection between individuals, events, or ideas help me better understand the text?	• What facts should I include in my informative/explanatory piece? • What reasons should I include to support my opinion?	
• How does the author's word choice impact my understanding of the text?	• How does my word choice impact my readers' understanding of my text?	• How does my word choice impact my listeners' understanding of my message?

Reading	Writing	Speaking/Listening
• How does the organization of a story/informational text help me understand the text?	• How do I organize a story? • How do I organize an informative/explanatory piece? • How do I organize an opinion piece?	• How do I organize my ideas?
• How does noticing and using text features help me understand the text?	• How do text features help my readers understand my writing?	• How does adding drawings and other visuals help my listeners understand?
• How does thinking about who is telling the story help me better understand the text?	• How do I show my point of view to my readers?	• How does thinking about the speaker's point of view help me understand the message?
• How does thinking about the author's purpose help me better understand the text?	• What am I trying to say to or teach my readers? How will my readers know?	• What is the speaker trying to say to or teach me? How do I know?
• How does using illustrations, details, and images help me better understand the text?	• How can I use illustrations, details, and images to present my ideas?	• How does adding drawings and other visuals help my listeners understand?
• What opinion is the author presenting? How do I know? • How do I know if the reasons the author gives effectively support the opinion?	• What makes for a good opinion piece? How can I get people to understand the thinking behind my opinion?	• What makes for a good opinion? How do I get people to understand the thinking behind my opinion?
• How does comparing and contrasting the approaches authors take help me better understand the text?	• What makes a good story? • What makes a good informational text?	• How do I share my thoughts, feelings, or ideas effectively?
• How does comparing and contrasting the approaches authors take help me better understand the topic?	• What makes a good informative/explanatory piece? • What questions do I want to answer about my topic? • How do I gather and select the best information to support my topic?	• How do I share facts that I know?
• How do I become a better reader?	• How do I strengthen my writing?	• How to do I expand my thinking?

Teach Reciprocal Processes

My colleagues and I have been working for a number of years to align our reading and writing instruction. In the charts that follow, you'll see how we align instruction. The first chart shows

 Transforming Literacy Teaching in the Era of Higher Standards, K–2 © 2015 by Maria P. Walther, Scholastic Teaching Resources

the reading strategies I teach in order to help the children better understand the writing genre we're studying.

Reading Strategies	Writing Genres
Schema, Making Connections	Personal Narrative
Predicting, Identifying Story Elements	Real/Make-Believe Stories
Questioning, Determining Importance	Biography
Mental Images, Inferring	Poetry
Determining Importance	Nonfiction

This chart shows how the reading skills and strategies align with the language of the writing traits.

Reading	Writing Traits
Schema/Connections	Ideas
Story Elements/Text Structures	Organization
Vocabulary	Word Choice
Fluency	Fluency
Author's Purpose	Voice (Audience/Purpose)
Conventions	Conventions

As I transform my teaching with today's more rigorous standards in mind, I know that I have to expand my definition of proficient literacy learners to include not only readers and writers, but also listeners and speakers. The chart on page 26 (Hallmarks of Proficient Literacy Learners) outlines my new thinking about the similarities in the reciprocal processes.

Read-Alouds That Demonstrate the Reading-Writing Connection

Cat Secrets (Czekaj, 2011)	If you are looking for an interactive read-aloud to engage young readers, reach for this humorous book where three felines try to determine if their readers are cats so that they can reveal their "Cat Secrets."
No Bears (McKinlay, 2011)	Ella wants to write the "prettiest, most exciting, scariest, and funniest book ever," and she believes that in order to accomplish this goal there must be no bears. What Ella doesn't realize is that a helpful bear that appears in the illustrations will save the day so that they can all live happily ever after.

Open Very Carefully: A Book With Bite (Bromley, 2013)	The ugly duckling finds a crocodile in the book he's reading aloud, and with the help of his fellow readers he rocks the crocodile to sleep—but not for long!
We Are in a Book (Willems, 2010)	Elephant and Piggie realize that they are, in fact, inside a book and someone is reading them. Together they discover the joy of being read!

Hallmarks of Proficient Literacy Learners

Proficient Readers/Listeners	Proficient Writers/Speakers
Construct meaning while reading by integrating and applying comprehension strategies and while listening by asking clarifying questions.	Convey meaning through writing or speaking by integrating and applying writing strategies and asking themselves questions to ensure the clarity of the message.
Search for text- or illustration-based evidence to support their understanding of the message.	Provide text- or illustration-based evidence to support their communication of the message.
Adjust their reading or listening based on their purpose, the genre, and type of text.	Design their written work to match their audience, task, purpose, and content.
Activate their schema and build background knowledge for a wide variety of texts.	Are active collectors of ideas and insights for writing and speaking through careful observation and wide reading.
Develop an understanding of how words work. (Foundational Skills)	Apply their growing knowledge of words as they stretch out words and spell them using the sounds they know.
Use decoding or fix-up strategies flexibly to figure out unknown words.	Apply strategies (word patterns, word endings, prefixes and suffixes, and so on) and utilize resources (word walls, environmental print, personal word banks, and the dictionary) to figure out how to spell words while writing.
Clarify the meaning of the vocabulary in the books they read or hear.	Choose precise, interesting words when they write and speak.
Use emerging knowledge of the conventions of standard English and grammar to help better understand the ideas of others.	Use emerging knowledge of the conventions of standard English and grammar when writing and speaking.
Read with fluency and expression.	Write and speak with fluency and expression.

(Adapted from Literature Is Back! *[Fuhler & Walther, 2007])*

As you work to transform your teaching, you are now armed with key concepts, essential questions, and a better understanding of the reciprocal literacy process of reading/listening and writing/speaking. Next, I'll share some common practices across all content areas that you can build as you and your students learn together.

Cultivate Beneficial Habits of Mind

Although I wrote this book to help you (and me!) better design our literacy instruction, we know as primary teachers that the more we can integrate across our day, the better. In the next section, I've synthesized and aligned the practices from math and science. Then, I matched the practices to my own set of English Language Arts (ELA) practices and clearly show how they, like the ELA standards, are interwoven and centered on key concepts. When you read through my chart (pages 28–30), you will clearly see that there is a common set of embedded thought processes that we can model, encourage, and celebrate across all subject areas.

Consider the hallmarks of proficient literacy learners.

I started by unpacking the Standards for Mathematical Practices (NGA Center/CCSSO, 2010, pp. 6–7). When I examined those practices, I saw habits of mind that we want to foster in our learners. These habits of mind are mirrored in The Next Generation Science Standards: Standards for Science and Engineering Practices (NGSS Lead States, 2013). I then created parallel literacy practices so that instead of looking at three separate sets of practices you have one set that can become part of the way your students think, act, and converse all day. In math, science, and engineering, we have moved away from "answer getting" or "fact memorization" toward thinking about what *mathematics, science, or engineering practices* the child can learn from solving a mathematical problem, answering

Integrate literacy across the day.

a scientific question, or defining/solving an engineering problem. Similarly, in literacy, we are helping learners discover what *enduring understandings* they can develop by comprehending the text or communicating with others that can transfer to future experiences. To assist you as you make these connections, you will find multi-genre text sets related to K–2 science topics on page 47. Below I've shared some of my favorite picture books to enhance your math experiences.

A Few of My Favorite Picture Books for Enhancing Math Understandings

Dog Loves Counting (Yates, 2013)	When Dog can't fall asleep, and counting sheep doesn't work, he opens a book looking for other interesting creatures to count including a five-lined skink and a nine-banded armadillo.
Lifetime: The Amazing Numbers in Animal Lives (Schaefer, 2013)	Did you know an alligator lays 550 eggs in one lifetime? This and other numerical facts about animals are shared in this unique counting book. The back matter provides more information about each animal, a lesson on calculating averages, and three story problems for students to solve.

Musk Ox Counts (Cabatingan, 2013)	Zebra is following Musk Ox through this humorous counting book trying to get him to return to his page.
The Wing Wing Brothers Carnival de Math (Long, 2013)	The Wing-Wing Brothers (whose names all begin with the letter *w*) enjoy three different carnival amusements while counting up and back to 100 by 10s. 

Our Air Experiment

Question: **What can air do?**

Hypothesis: Air makes wind.

Materials: balloon, feather, straw, paper, cotton ball, styrofoam ball

Experiment: See what air can do

Results:
* Heavier things fall faster
* Trapped air comes out fast
* Air can make things get bigger (expand)
* Air moves things
* Air can help make noise
* Air makes wind.

Conclusion: Air makes wind!

Guide learners as they answer scientific questions.

Common Core Standards for Mathematical Practice	The Next Generation Science Standards: Standards for Science and Engineering Practices (K–2)	Maria's Standards for Literacy Practices
Make sense of problems and persevere in solving them. Mathematically proficient students figure out the meaning of the problem and look for various ways to solve it. They think about similar problems that might help them solve the problem (the way using spelling patterns and analogies helps readers decode words). As they are working, they monitor and evaluate their progress toward solving the problem (similar to self-monitoring in reading). Finally, they check their answer to the problem using a different method (cross-checking). Learners continually ask themselves, "Does this make sense?" "If not, what can I do to figure this out?"	**Make sense of the natural and engineered world and persevere in figuring it out.** Young scientists and engineers try to figure out more about the natural and designed world. To do this, they ask or identify simple, descriptive questions that they can investigate. Young engineers attempt to solve problems by developing new or improved objects or tools. Learners continually ask themselves, "How can I make sense of my world? What can I do to figure it out?" *(Adapted from Practice #1, Asking Questions and Defining Problems)*	**Make sense of words and persevere in figuring them out.** Proficient readers and listeners figure out the meaning of words at many different levels. They independently integrate and apply strategies to decode words, figure out the meaning of words, and understand what the author/speaker is trying to say with those words. To confirm their understanding and check for misconceptions, they compare their schema with their new learning. Then they consider what they think about the message and any actions they want to take after hearing/reading the words. Learners continually ask themselves, "Does this make sense?" "If not, what can I do to figure this out?"

Transforming Literacy Teaching in the Era of Higher Standards, K–2 © 2015 by Maria P. Walther, Scholastic Teaching Resources

Common Core Standards for Mathematical Practice	The Next Generation Science Standards: Standards for Science and Engineering Practices (K–2)	Maria's Standards for Literacy Practices
Reason abstractly and quantitatively. Learners who are mathematically proficient "make sense of quantities and their relationships in problem situations." Using quantitative reasoning means that students can attend to the meaning of the quantities, not just how to compute quantities.	**Reason analytically and interpret patterns and relationships.** Skilled scientists and engineers observe, collect and record data, and share observations with others. Reasoning analytically means that students are able to use observations and data to answer scientific questions, solve problems, or determine if an object or tool worked. *(Adapted from #4, Analyzing and Interpreting Data)*	**Reason abstractly and qualitatively.** Proficient learners are able to understand, problem solve, and plan based on information gained from text and/or images. Using qualitative reasoning means students can attend to the meaning of the words, not just how to decode the words.
Construct viable arguments and critique the reasoning of others. Children in the early grades can show how they've solved the mathematical problem using objects, drawings, diagrams, and actions while their classmates listen, decide whether their argument makes sense, and ask helpful questions to clarify or strengthen their argument. Constructing and critiquing arguments helps learners confirm or revise their thinking.	**Construct and recognize evidence-based arguments and critique the reasoning of others.** Experienced scientists and engineers are able to make a claim about an object, tool, or solution and support that claim with evidence rather than opinion. As scientific learners, they are able to identify evidence-supported arguments and figure out why some evidence is relevant to the scientific question and some is not. They also actively listen to arguments, state whether they agree or disagree, and explain their thinking. *(Adapted from #7, Engaging in Argument From Evidence)*	**Construct logical, evidence-based arguments and critique the reasoning of others.** Proficient writers and speakers may add actions, drawings, or visual displays that include text- or illustration-based evidence to their descriptions to clarify ideas, thoughts, and feelings. Then, as listeners, they ask questions to clear up confusions about topics, deepen understanding, gather additional information, and/or clarify comprehension. Constructing and critiquing evidence-based arguments helps learners confirm or revise their thinking.
Model with mathematics. Skilled mathematicians apply mathematics to solve problems that occur in everyday life, school, and the larger community. They show the relationship among identified quantities using tools such as diagrams, tables, and graphs. Then, they analyze the relationships mathematically to draw conclusions asking themselves, "Do the results make sense in this context?"	**Develop and use models.** Budding scientists develop models to solve problems in the natural and designed world. They are able to distinguish between the drawing, replica, or diorama and the real event or model it represents. They ask themselves, "How is what I learned from studying this model going to help me to better understand what it represents?" *(Adapted from #2, Developing and Using Models)*	**Think by writing.** In literacy, students clarify their thinking by writing or drawing. To compare and contrast two books or characters, learners might create a Venn diagram or H-Chart and then analyze the relationship between the two. They may use two-column notes to record their schema and new learning, always asking themselves, "How is what I learned by writing this down going to help me as a reader?"

Common Core Standards for Mathematical Practice	The Next Generation Science Standards: Standards for Science and Engineering Practices (K–2)	Maria's Standards for Literacy Practices
Use appropriate tools strategically. To explore and deepen their understanding of concepts, mathematical learners strategically select the best available tools, such as pencil and paper, a model, rulers, or technological tools, to help them solve the problem. They make decisions about which tool might be helpful along with its limitations. In addition, they check to see if they've correctly used the tool.	**Use mathematical and computational thinking strategically.** To describe the natural and designed world, young scientists and engineers strategically select the best type of data to use when describing patterns, comparing attributes, or considering alternative solutions to a problem. *(Adapted from Practice #5, Using Mathematical and Computational Thinking)*	**Use structures of text, text features, and digital resources strategically.** To enhance their understanding of a text, literacy learners think about the structure of the text. For example, if the text is a story, they know to expect characters, settings, and major events. When reading a nonfiction text, they will use text features to learn additional information not provided in the running text. When accessing information on the Internet, they'll understand how to use icons and electronic menus to efficiently locate facts or key information.
Construct precise explanations. Mathematically proficient learners work to communicate precisely to their classmates. To do this, they give carefully formulated explanations to each other.	**Construct explanations and design solutions.** To construct an evidence-based account of a natural occurrence or design solutions, accomplished scientists carefully observe. In order to solve a problem, engineers design or build a device. In addition, engineers compare multiple solutions to determine the most effective one. *(Adapted from practice #6, Attend to Precision)*	**Comprehend and communicate with precision.** To better comprehend the text they are reading, accomplished readers attend to precision by using context clues to confirm or self-correct, reread, and self-monitor as readers. In order to communicate their ideas effectively, they use their knowledge of language and conventions when they are writing or speaking.
Look for and make use of structure and express regularity in repeated reasoning. Mathematical problem solvers try to figure out how structure and patterns can help them solve a problem. To assist them in this quest, they look for patterns, sort, and categorize. Mathematicians will understand that patterns show relationships that exist in real life. To do this, they notice if calculations are repeated and look for general methods and short cuts. They pay attention to the big picture while attending to the details and evaluate reasonableness of their results.	**Look for and make use of structure.** Scientists use observation, along with counting and numbers, to identify and describe patterns. Then they use models to represent patterns found in the natural or designed world.	**Look for and make use of structure.** Literacy learners try to figure out how structure and patterns can help them better understand words, texts, and ideas. To do this, they may sort words into categories to better understand the meaning of the words, and/or use context clues and word clues (root words, prefixes, and suffixes) to figure out unknown words. Adept literacy learners know that patterns exist in language and in life. They pay attention to meaning while attending to words. In addition, they are continually self-monitoring to evaluate their understanding.

 Transforming Literacy Teaching in the Era of Higher Standards, K–2 © 2015 by Maria P. Walther, Scholastic Teaching Resources

Again, the goal here is to gain an understanding of the common threads running across the practices so that when you are faced with a teachable moment you can seize the opportunity to utilize the practices. For example, consider the practice of looking for and making use of structure or patterns. Think about how many times during a day you and your students look for and use patterns. In reading workshop, your students look for patterns at the end of words to determine whether they are C-V-C (short vowel) words or C-V-C-E (long vowel/silent *e*) words. During math, you are looking at patterns on a hundreds grid to help students locate even numbers. Later, young scientists study the patterns of motion of the sun across the sky. It takes just an extra moment to make that connection for your learners. To recap at the end of the day, you might say something like, "Wow! We used a lot of different patterns today! Can you share a pattern that you used and how it helped you as a learner?"

Think about how many times during a day you and your students look for and use patterns.

SYNTHESIZE LEARNING TARGETS

I don't know about you, but when I glance back over all of the practices and think about the youngsters in our classes, I get a little overwhelmed. When I get overwhelmed, I try to step back and search for ways to simplify. Now that you have a better understanding of each of the individual practices, you can communicate them to young learners using the following learning targets:

- I can PAUSE.
- I can PONDER.
- I can look for PATTERNS.
- I can PROBLEM SOLVE.
- I can be PRECISE.
- I can communicate my PROCESS.
- I can PERSEVERE.

As the year progresses, you can highlight each learning target by providing concrete examples and a lot of modeling. Of all of the learning targets, the one I like to tackle first is perseverance. So often young learners are used to getting things "right" or "done" the first time. Perseverance is linked to so many of the habits we are trying to instill in our students, habits that call for sustained attention and focus, even when it's challenging! Whether it's figuring out an unknown word, building stamina for independent reading, or sounding out words while writing, perseverance is the key. To clarify this concept, I begin by reading books with characters that demonstrate perseverance. Then, I look for opportunities during the day to point out and celebrate students who work at something even when it is challenging.

Text Set of Picture Books With Characters Who Persevere

❋ *Clever Jack Takes the Cake* (Fleming, 2010)

❋ *Cloudette* (Lichtenheld, 2011)
❋ *The Dot* (Reynolds, 2003)
❋ *The Little Engine That Could* (Piper, 1930)
❋ *Superdog: The Heart of a Hero* (Buehner, 2004)
❋ *Today I Will Fly!* (Willems, 2007)
❋ *Winners Never Quit* (Hamm, 2004)
❋ *Wolf!* (Bloom, 1999)

We've discovered the connections among the English Language Arts standards for reading, writing, listening, and speaking. We revisited the reciprocal relationships between reading and writing, and we synthesized the practices that learners use as mathematicians, scientists, engineers, and literate citizens. Next, we'll consider how science and engineering practices align with writing standards and how you can integrate the writing standards into your science instruction or vise versa.

INTEGRATE INVESTIGATION, RESEARCH, AND WRITING

I hope that by now your "big picture" of the standards is growing and you are able to see connections not only among the ELA standards, but also across the content-area practices. I'd like to propose one last connection to consider as you transform your teaching. These are what I like to call the inquiry-focused practices and standards. In their book *Comprehension and Collaboration: Inquiry Circles in Action* (2009), Stephanie Harvey and Harvey Daniels define the inquiry approach to teaching by identifying the following three key strands (pp. 56–57):

- Framing school study around questions developed and shaped by kids

- Handing the brainwork of learning back to the kids

- Focusing on the development of kids' thinking, first, foremost, and always

With instructional minutes at a premium and with a goal of helping students attain true understanding, it makes sense to integrate your shared research and writing projects with the investigations your children are doing in science. So in addition to immersing students in the genre of personal narrative or opinion writing, you can combine your writing workshop time with the minutes you allocate for science instruction and immerse students in inquiry units to support them as they investigate, research, and write.

Support students as they investigate, research, and write.

Take a moment to read through the Next Generation Science Practices 3 and 8 (www.nextgenscience.org) and compare them with the ELA Writing Standards 7 and 8 (www.corestandards.org/ELA-Literacy); you will discover that there are the following shared expectations for students' learning:

- Participate in shared or collaborative investigations or research to answer questions or support an idea.

- Gather information from multiple resources such as texts, images, investigations, or experiences to answer a question or solve a problem.

- Recall information from multiple resources such as texts, images, investigations, or experiences to answer a question or solve a problem.

- Evaluate different ways to observe and measure or different sources of information to determine the best way or resource to help answer the question.

Offer opportunities for students to communicate information in diagrams.

- Communicate new information or ideas orally or in writing using details such as models, diagrams, drawings, and/or text features.

The Four Stages of Small-Group Inquiry

IMMERSE	INVESTIGATE	COALESCE	GO PUBLIC
• Invite curiosity • Build background • Find topics • Wonder	• Develop questions • Search for information • Discover answers	• Intensify research • Synthesize information • Build knowledge	• Share learning • Demonstrate understanding • Take action

(Harvey & Daniels, 2009, pp. 61–62)

When you compare these expectations with the four stages of inquiry that appear in the box above, it is clear that the inquiry approach is essential in helping children meet these standards.

If we want our students to be self-directed and independent learners, we have to create learning opportunities where they can investigate their own questions or test out their own theories and ideas. As difficult as it may be with young learners, we must step aside and let children take their first wobbly steps down this path to understanding. After all, we want our students to leave our classrooms knowing that if they have questions about the world around them they also have the skills and strategies needed to begin to answer those questions themselves. How, then, do we set up those learning experiences? I believe it is by refocusing some of our current teaching practices to transform them into inquiry experiences.

Transform Teaching Routines and Create Inquiry Experiences

As I've said to the many teachers and administrators I've mentored in transforming their practices to meet higher standards, I believe most primary teachers understand the roots of effective English Language Arts teaching, and have for many years. Because we teach everything, we've always searched for ways to integrate instruction and provide time for students to dig deeper. Teachers of young children recognize the social nature of learning and the importance of talk.

We value and celebrate approximation, trusting that with our descriptive feedback and scaffolding it will lead to true understanding. We know that foundational skills are essential to becoming proficient readers, but also are aware that these fundamental skills should be integrated and taught in meaningful ways. Because of this, we already have research-based routines like the ones shown in the box on page 34 in our current instructional repertoire.

Design learning opportunities where students can investigate their own questions.

Recognize the social nature of learning and the importance of talk.

In Chapters 3, 4, and 5, I will reexamine each of these routines and offer suggestions for transforming them in order to nudge students toward independence by changing the focus along with the language, questions, and conversation that surround it.

Unfortunately, in many schools around this country, this deep knowledge of early childhood learning is not valued. Instead, teachers are handed packaged program after packaged program to ensure that everyone is "on the same page" both literally and figuratively. If I were in charge of the education world, I'd take the millions currently spent on packaged programs and allocate it to high-quality professional development and an abundance of text. Luckily, you've already decided to engage in your own personal professional development by reading this book, and you'll soon learn how to transform familiar teaching routines and add another layer on top. This layer consists of inquiry experiences.

My definition of an inquiry experience is a learning context or learning opportunity that is intentionally planned so that, over time, students internalize and independently apply the literacy practices that I developed earlier in this chapter and that are recapped below.

Research-Based Routines

READING

❋ Read aloud

❋ Think aloud

❋ Mini-lessons

❋ Shared reading

❋ Interactive reading

❋ Independent reading

WRITING

❋ Read aloud like a writer

❋ Write aloud (writing demonstrations)

❋ Mini-lessons

❋ Shared writing

❋ Interactive writing

❋ Independent writing

Maria's Standards for Literacy Practices

- Make sense of words and persevere in figuring them out.
- Reason abstractly and qualitatively.
- Construct logical, evidence-based arguments and critique the reasoning of others.
- Think by writing.
- Use structures of text, text features, and digital resources strategically.
- Comprehend and communicate with precision.
- Look for and make use of structure.

Coach, guide, and give descriptive feedback.

To plan an inquiry experience, begin by asking yourself, "What do I want my students to know and be able to do once they've been immersed in the learning?" *Each learning experience can and should be repeated over the course of the year with increasingly more complex texts or ideas.* These inquiry experiences are not "one and done" lessons to check off a list. Rather, they comprise a way of teaching the standards that is authentic and integrated into your daily instruction—as opposed to disconnected, or as I call them "cute," activities. This is where the Transforming Teaching charts will come in handy. In Part 2, I'll show you how you can refine your teaching routines and create inquiry experiences that better align with the standards, thinking practices, and community-building ideas we've already discussed.

Transforming Literacy Teaching in the Era of Higher Standards, K–2 © 2015 by Maria P. Walther, Scholastic Teaching Resources

The Characteristics of Inquiry Experiences	The Steps to Creating Inquiry Experiences
• Deepen students' ability to integrate and apply reading, writing, thinking, listening, and speaking skills. • Expand learners' understanding of the world. • Encourage inquiry, uncertainty, risk-taking, and perseverance. • Develop agency, also known as an "I can do this myself" attitude. • Emphasize text-based evidence to support ideas, thinking, and writing. • Foster understandings about complex texts and ideas. • Promote joyful learning.	• Determine learning targets to lead students toward key understandings that are rooted in the essential questions derived from the standards (see page 23). • Select the experience that best meets the target and matches your students' needs. • Demonstrate, coach, guide, observe, give descriptive feedback, take anecdotal notes, and collect formative assessment data. • Create opportunities to authentically assess your learners' understanding of the target. • Reflect and repeat!

To further strengthen your transformed teaching practices and to help students achieve the more rigorous standards, I suggest incorporating formative assessment. Formative assessment is powerful because it helps you gain a better understanding of students' understandings and/or misconceptions, it offers opportunities to give the descriptive feedback necessary to nudge students forward, and it helps students begin to self-assess and reflect on their own learning and progress.

Utilize Formative Assessment

I've been assessing and teaching young learners for over a quarter of a century, so you could say I've "done it all" in terms of using assessment to guide the instructional choices I make in my classroom. During my first years of teaching, I taught with a teacher named Joan, who told me that in order to form her "reading groups" (yes, those were the days of three reading groups) she simply said the following to her first graders: "If you can read a lot of words, go over there. If you can read a few words, walk to the other side of the room. If you can't read at all, stay here in the middle." When I reflect on that conversation, I still smile. Then, I pause and ponder. What is the purpose of assessment? If the purpose of assessment is to learn more about our students so that we can meet them where they are and provide instructional opportunities that will take them further, then Joan was on the right track. She began by pre-assessing her students' perceptions of themselves as readers. To be clear, I'm not advocating the simplistic approach Joan used to form her reading groups, but it does remind us about the importance of focusing on *the child*.

Certainly, you know that by the time children walk through our classroom doors, they have started to develop their reading and writing identities based on their interactions with family members, teachers, and other influential people in their lives. They have developed a sense of whether or not they believe they can read and write. The next steps for Joan would be to uncover the other aspects of her students' literacy knowledge by finding out more about their understanding of how letters and words work and whether they can put their thoughts into written words. She would discover more about their ability to read accurately and fluently in order to comprehend, converse, and write about their reading,

Use assessment data to determine a student's specific strengths and weaknesses.

Big Ideas About Formative Assessment

�֍ Formative assessment is an ongoing, reflective process.

✖ Formative assessment will help you answer the following questions, which are critical to effective literacy instruction:

- What are my students' strengths and weaknesses?

- How should I group children to maximize learning?

- What specific, descriptive feedback should I give each learner?

- What adjustments should I make to my instruction?

✖ Formative assessment maximizes both motivation and achievement by giving students the tools they need to set goals, reflect on progress, and self-assess. Through your interactions with students, you are guiding them to ask these questions:

- Where am I going?

- Where am I now?

- How can I close the gap?

(Chappuis, 2009, p. 9)

their budding interests, and their misconceptions. So, in order to prepare to teach a child, we ask ourselves three big questions (Chappuis, 2009):

- Where do I want this learner to end up?

- Where is the student right now?

- How can I close the gap?

To answer the first question, "Where do I want this learner to end up?" we return to the portrait of a learner described in Chapter 1, along with the specific standards for our grade level, and from there we *identify learning targets*. We answer the second question, "Where is the student right now?" when we *check for understanding* using notes taken during collaborative conversations, anecdotal notes, classroom tasks, and other assessment data or processes to identify a student's specific strengths and weaknesses. I will elaborate on each of these below. Then, we deliberately link the information we gain from those assessments to drive our instruction while guiding learners as a whole class, individually, and in small groups. For some big ideas related to formative assessment, see the box at left. If you are interested in more detailed information on formative assessment, I would recommend Jan Chappuis' book *Seven Strategies of Assessment for Learning* (2009). Finally, the crucial third question, "How Can I Close the Gap?" is answered when teachers *design powerful inquiry experiences* that address each student's specific learning needs. To help students better understand where we want them to end up, each teaching routine and inquiry experience should be driven by a learning target or targets.

If you're new to formative assessment, the following are some helpful tips I found in an article entitled "Formative Assessment: Simply, No Additives" (Roskos & Neuman, 2012).

- Select multi-level activities with clear learning targets that involve text-learner as well as teacher-student interactions for formative assessments.

- Embed key concepts (ideas or principles central to mastery) and skills (procedures or strategies essential to performance) in the content of the activity.

- Determine success criteria for the activity, often detailed in the form of a rubric.

- Create a schedule or plan for completing assessments.

- Start slow, adding activities as your expertise grows (this is my addition to their steps!).

Transforming Literacy Teaching in the Era of Higher Standards, K–2 © 2015 by Maria P. Walther, Scholastic Teaching Resources

IDENTIFY LEARNING TARGETS

In Part 2 of this book, I've identified possible student-friendly learning targets for each teaching routine and inquiry experience. When I created each learning target, I began by unpacking the standard or thinking about the prerequisite understandings, skills, or concepts the child would have to possess to attain that particular standard. Taking time to identify and define learning targets is a beneficial activity to do in your professional learning community. I then translated each learning target into a kid-friendly "I can" statement by using language young students can understand. These learning targets provide a clear and understandable vision of the purpose of the learning experience. As you begin to create your own learning targets, remember to keep them balanced across the year, including knowledge, strategy, reasoning, and demonstration-of-understanding learning targets for children (Miller, 2013a; Chappuis, 2009). The next step is to create sensible, time-efficient ways to determine the students' current state of learning or understanding in order to answer the question, "Where is the student right now?"

CHECK FOR UNDERSTANDING

Clear learning targets narrow our focus, shape the assessments we use to check for understanding, and guide students as they reflect on their own learning. We continually check for understanding by kid-watching. In fact, we are expert kid watchers. I'll bet you know by the end of your first week of school which students are struggling, which learners will need some extra challenges, who needs to work on attention and focus, and who needs modeling, prompting, and reinforcement to demonstrate expected behaviors. (In fact, you probably know who they are on Day 1!) How do we transform kid-watching into anecdotal data, give descriptive feedback, and move students forward? The following are just a few ways to collect anecdotal data as you check students' understanding of the learning targets you've set forth.

- Listen and take notes in your teaching notebook as students think and share.
- Record students' thinking and ideas on anchor charts.
- Create a system for taking conferring notes.
- Use exit slips to assess specific skills.
- Analyze students' written responses.

In Part 2, you'll find plenty of learning experiences where you can use these data collection techniques.

Looking Back, Moving Forward

In Chapter 1, you learned the conditions that work together to create a learning environment where agency and independence are cultivated and celebrated. In Chapter 2, we added a layer to those conditions by examining the intertwining of content-area standards, the definition of inquiry experiences, and the role of formative assessment in the development of a learner. In the next two chapters, we'll move forward by revisiting two learning contexts, reading workshop (Chapter 3) and writing workshop (Chapter 4), to integrate what we've learned so far in order to elevate and enhance these research-based structures.

Chapter 3

Elevating Reading Workshop

The More We Read, the Better We Get

As I put the finishing touches on this book, I celebrated my 50th birthday and wrapped up my 28th year of teaching first grade. When I reflect on the decades I've spent immersed in professional learning, writing, and daily teaching, I clearly see that, for me, there has been one constant, unwavering belief—in the power of books and reading. And that's because, as I tell my first graders, the "secret" to becoming an even better reader is simple: "The more you read, the better you get!" In this chapter, I'll review the conditions and components that will elevate your reading workshop and unleash the power of books.

Go online to view a video on Reading Workshop in Action; see page 160.

Workshop Conditions

My husband, Lenny, is a woodworker. He spends many long days in his basement workshop sawing and sanding as I sit in my office above writing (often with my headphones on!). Sometimes I wonder what he does all day long. Then, I remind myself that, basically, he is creating something out of nothing. Crafting anything takes time, trial and error, and in his case, many trips to the hardware store. Our house is strewn with woodworking magazines and ideas for future projects. He also connects with his fellow craftsmen in person and through electronic media. Let's explore the concept of a workshop to discover how Lenny's time in his basement workshop mirrors the workshops we create in our classrooms. The following conditions are essential to creating a dynamic workshop environment:

- Time
- Materials
- Choice
- Structure
- Mentor or Expert Support

Together, these conditions support learners in becoming proficient, independent, and motivated readers. Here I will share a bit more about each of the conditions and give you tips for creating them in your classroom.

Time

It seems to take a long time for my husband to complete a project. Often, I tease him about this, but when I finally see the finished product I know it was worth the wait. Although our youngest readers are working on a project that will never be quite "finished," we expect that it is going to take them time (some longer than others) to learn how to make meaning out of letters, sounds, and words. Breaking the code takes trial and error and ample *time* to practice. All of our readers, especially those who are developing, must have ample time each day to engage in "high-success" reading. Children are engaged in high-success reading when they can read the text with 98% accuracy or better (Allington, 2013). That's why a workshop is designed to include time for independent reading—to allow students to apply the skills acquired during teaching routines like read-alouds and mini-lessons. At right, you will find two sample reading workshop schedules showing how you might divide your allotted time between the different components. Note that as your learners' stamina builds over the course of the year, the

Provide ample time each day for students to engage in "high-success" reading.

Sample 60-Minute Reading Workshop Schedule

5– 10 minutes	Read-Aloud/Whole-Group Mini-Lesson
5– 15 minutes	Independent Reading/ Guiding Readers: Conferring (2–3 children per day)
5– 30 minutes	Explore the W. O. R. L. D./ Guiding Readers in Small Groups (2 groups per day)
5 minutes	Sharing and Celebrating

Sample 90-Minute Reading Workshop Schedule

5– 10 minutes	Read-Aloud/Whole-Group Mini-Lesson #1
5– 25 minutes	Independent Reading/ Guiding Readers: Conferring (3–5 children per day)
5– 10 minutes	Read-Aloud/Whole-Group Mini-Lesson #2
5– 40 minutes	Explore the W. O. R. L. D./ Guiding Readers in Small Groups (2–3 groups per day)
5 minutes	Sharing and Celebrating

time they spend reading independently or working in literacy-related centers, workstations—or as we call it, Explore the W. O. R. L. D. (Walther & Phillips, 2012)—will grow.

Materials

In order for the workshop time to run smoothly, children need well-organized materials that are matched to their interests and learning needs. Just as Lenny's workshop is filled with the tools and raw materials he needs to complete a particular project (apparently you can never have too many clamps), a workshop classroom is designed to have readily accessible materials displayed in organized and kid-friendly ways. Then children can independently locate the materials they need and store them when they are finished. When learners know where to find what they need they are better able to use their time wisely. The most abundant material you will need to elevate your workshop is, of course, books! Additionally, it is important to collect and locate other types of texts, including digital resources. To keep students' books organized and easily accessible, I divide them into categories and have different shelves and baskets around our classroom to house each kind of book. This is helpful when teaching about different genres, focusing on books written by a particular author, or finding the perfect book for a reluctant reader. Here are some ways you might choose to organize your own classroom library:

- **ABC Shelves**—Organized in alphabetical order by author's last name and housed on A-Frame shelves where students can see the covers of the books.

- **Author/Series Baskets**—Separated in baskets for different authors or series like Dr. Seuss, Eric Carle, Elephant and Piggie, or Fly Guy.

- **Nonfiction Shelves**—Categorized by the topics studied in science and social studies.

- **Dot Baskets**—Leveled according to Fountas & Pinnell's (2009), alphabetic leveling system. Each book has a corresponding colored dot to indicate the level.

ABC Shelf

Author/Series Baskets

Nonfiction Shelves

Dot Baskets

Seasonal Shelf

Genre Baskets

- **Seasonal Shelf**—Changed each month to reflect the holidays or other topics highlighted that particular month.

- **Genre Baskets**—Sorted in baskets for primary-grade genres like ABC Books, Wordless Books, Song Picture Books, Traditional Tales, Graphic Novels, and so on.

As you introduce the different materials in your classroom, it is essential that you plan time to teach a mini-lesson on how to take care of that particular material. An anchor chart listing the expected behaviors when using each material is helpful for students who benefit from additional reteaching, prompting, and support throughout the year.

Choice

People often ask Lenny why he doesn't sell the things he makes in his workshop. He answers simply, "Because it would no longer be fun." He enjoys the variety of making different items for friends and relatives to celebrate special events and crafting items for us to use around our house—it's his choice. Choice is the key for kids, too. We know that a child's motivation and willingness to tackle more complex texts increases when he or she is interested in the topic or text (Optiz, Ford, & Erekson, 2011). I've found that young readers often haven't had enough exposure to a wide variety of texts to really know yet what kinds of texts they like. That's why I start my year by giving the reading interest survey found in the *Next Step Guided Reading Assessment* (Richardson & Walther, 2013). This grade-level specific survey zeroes in on students' overall interests by simply asking them to identify topics of interest—like sharks, princesses, or superheroes. Then, I can use this information to guide my text selection for read-alouds and small-group instruction, or to gather a variety of texts at a child's independent level that build on or support his or her interests.

Pair students to discuss their reading interest surveys.

Take Anna, for example. Anna was interested in famous people. So I put books in her hands about people she already knew, and as her confidence and reading ability grew, I challenged her to read about less familiar people like Helen Keller and Rosa Parks. Then, with my support, she branched out further to include historical events such as the sinking of the *Titanic*, an event she learned a lot about. From Regie Routman (2008) I learned the importance of choice within structure. Predictable routines, structure, and clear expectations, along with lots of modeling and process-oriented feedback, are essential when helping children make thoughtful choices about their actions and their learning.

Put books in students' hands that match their interests.

Structure

There is a fine line between just enough structure and too much of it. Personally, I still struggle with "letting go" and have had to work over the years to step back and encourage my students to take the lead. As a result, I've become skilled at putting routines in place that facilitate independent learning, and I can share the following tips:

- **Be prepared.** My best teaching days are the ones when I have everything I need at my fingertips, because then we can move fluidly from one activity to the next. Being prepared for reading workshop means having read-aloud texts handy (I have an "on deck" easel or book box where I keep those at the ready), chart paper and markers (or an interactive whiteboard document) to record students' thinking, and a plan of whom I would like to confer with and/or which guided reading groups I'll be meeting with that day.

Have your read-aloud texts handy.

- **Be flexible.** I'm not sure which is more important, being prepared or being flexible. Teachable moments only happen if you're flexible. For instance, if a collaborative conversation is going well, let the talking continue. If a child needs a bit of extra support, spend a few additional minutes conferring with him or her. Being flexible and capitalizing on teachable moments means that you don't always accomplish what you've planned for the day or week. Some might say, "I can't do that or I'll fall behind." My response to that is, "Behind what?" If you forge ahead because it's written in your plan book or your colleagues are on the next topic or big idea, you're probably leaving some students behind. Let your students' needs and successes serve as your measure for how much you've accomplished, not a publisher's program or someone else's agenda or plan.

- **Be present.** I began teaching long before the arrival of the "immediate response" world. Back then, if parents wanted to talk with me, they would send a note or call the office to leave a message. They would never expect me to return their call during the school day while I was busy teaching their children. (I didn't even have a phone in my classroom!) Now, everyone expects us to check our e-mail and respond while teaching. Although teachers are multi-tasking masters, it is difficult to be present in an interaction with a child when you're thinking about a parent's e-mail that you saw when you glanced at your computer. For me, being present means tuning out the rest of the world and focusing on the children and their needs when I'm with them; I tackle the e-mails and other tasks during my planning time. Just as you can tell when a student is not really listening to you, children can sense when you're not present.

Mentor or Expert Support

The final condition in cultivating a workshop environment is you! For Lenny, woodworking magazines, television shows, and chatting with fellow craftsmen provide support as he hones his craft. In the classroom, we, along with their classmates, are the mentors who provide readers with the descriptive feedback and strategy-specific prompts that nudge them toward independence. Standard 10 clearly states that children will be able to read grade-level texts *with prompting and support* (Grade 1) and *with scaffolding as needed* at the high end of the range (Grade 2). One of the many misconceptions related to the standards is that children in the primary grades don't need scaffolded support as they tackle complex texts. If you've worked with primary-grade readers for any length of time, I don't have to tell you how ridiculous this sounds. Of course, we have to support our readers as they move through the stages of reading development. With enough time, well-selected materials, strategic choices, purposeful structure, and you as their mentor, students will be able to meet or exceed expectations. Your expertise is the critical factor in the quality of the reading lessons your children will receive (Stuhlman & Pianta, 2009). Mentoring young children into the world of reading is one of the most rewarding aspects of our profession.

Workshop Components

How do we set up a reading workshop that not only meets these conditions, but also incorporates recent research about the importance of teacher language and environment (Chapter 1) and the integrated standards-based practices (Chapter 2) that will elevate our current workshop to help students attain the goals set forth in the standards? We reflect on where we are and consider how we might move forward. In the Transforming Teaching chart below, I've outlined the instructional shifts necessary to elevate the reading workshop. I will address each shift as I review the components of a K–2 reading workshop.

TRANSFORMING TEACHING	
The selection of books used for read-alouds, guided reading, and independent reading is somewhat random.	The selection of books—some organized by text sets and ordered using a ladder of complexity (Biggs-Tucker & Tucker, 2015) —is intentional.
Texts are mainly fiction with some nonfiction integrated here and there.	Informational texts play a more prominent role.
Two-way conversations—teacher-student, student-student—are most prevalent.	Collaborative conversations initiated by students in response to peers' questions, thoughts, and opinions permeate the day.
Reading responses are based on prior knowledge and experiences.	Reading responses are based on prior knowledge and experience coupled with text-based evidence.
Separate mini-lessons are based on individual strategies and skills from state standards, district curriculum, or packaged program scope and sequence.	A series of mini-lessons is centered on big ideas integrated across language arts strands (reading, writing, speaking, listening, viewing/visually representing).
Comprehension strategies are the organizing feature.	Overarching themes and big ideas are the organizing feature; comprehension strategies are used as tools to better understand text.
Guided reading is seen as a "one size fits all" venture.	Teachers guide readers in many different ways. In small groups, the instructional focus and content of guided-reading lessons changes based on students' level of reading development and, if needed, includes word study and guided writing.
Everyone, including the teacher, reads during D. E. A. R. (Drop Everything and Read) or S. S. R. (Sustained Silent Reading).	Teachers surround "independent" reading by actively structuring conditions, such as explicit instruction and teacher monitoring, to increase students' accountability and progress toward reading more complex texts.
Sharing is focused on *what* readers did or learned.	Sharing and celebration are focused on reflections about *how* readers went about learning—the process or strategies that were independently applied.

As I shared in Chapter 2, each component of the reading workshop, when planned with the standards in mind, can be transformed to benefit your students. In this chapter, I'll review the building blocks of a workshop and share how to elevate each part by making strategic instructional moves. Then, in Part 2, you'll find specific teaching routines and inquiry experiences that address various components for each reading standard. As you read through the components in the box below, view them as a menu rather than a checklist. I learned this stress-saving tip from Sharon Taberski's *Comprehension From the Ground Up* (2011). Although read-alouds, independent reading, guided reading, and sharing should take place every day, the remaining elements may not. Depending on your students and your teaching focus, you might choose to spend a bit more time one day on having a collaborative conversation and the next day on a reading response. Your professional decision-making is key to balancing the different aspects of the workshop effectively.

I've always been a proponent of the menu approach to teaching. I also believe that providing students with menus is just one way to offer choice within structure. For example, you might say something like, "Today during independent reading you can read books from your book box, the nonfiction shelves, or the author baskets." The expectation or structure is that everyone will be reading independently, the choice is the type of book students select.

A Quick Look at the Components of a K–2 Reading Workshop

❊ Read-Alouds

❊ Collaborative Conversations

❊ Reading Response

❊ Mini-Lessons

  • Embedded Comprehension Strategy Instruction

  • Foundational Skills Instruction: Word Recognition and Fluency

  • Language Instruction: Grammar and Vocabulary

❊ Guiding Readers Individually and/or in Small Groups

❊ "Independent" Reading

❊ Sharing and Celebrating

Read Aloud

Develop Text Sets ⟶ *The selection of books—some organized by text sets and ordered using a ladder of complexity (Biggs-Tucker & Tucker, 2015)—is intentional.*

Incorporate Informational Texts ⟶ *Informational texts play a more prominent role.*

One of my earliest mentors in the field of education was my undergraduate language arts professor at Northern Illinois University, Dr. Pamela Farris. I can still see Pam walking into the room with a suitcase full of books and beginning our very first course together by saying, "Join me for a story." She started each class session this way and continued to do that throughout my many (many) years at NIU. Each semester, we went on a field trip to an independent bookseller housed in the homeowner/children's literature experts' basement in DeKalb, IL. From Pam, I learned the power of a read-aloud to engage, teach, calm, excite, and bring together a group of people around a shared book experience. I'm always hopeful that our read-aloud time is one of the things my students will remember about their year in my classroom. With the increased emphasis on higher-level thinking and understanding of complex texts, read-alouds play a prominent role across our school day and especially in the reading workshop. That fact is underscored by the authors of the Common Core State Standards when they say, "By reading a story or nonfiction selection aloud, teachers allow children to experience written language without the burden of decoding, granting them access to the content that they may not be able to read and understand by themselves. Children are then free to focus their mental energy on the words and ideas presented in the text, and they will eventually be better prepared to tackle rich written content on their own" (CCSS, p. 27). Here I will highlight three ways to elevate the read-aloud experience during reading workshop:

- Develop text sets.

- Incorporate informational texts.

- Provide lots of support.

Later, in Chapter 5, I'll show you how to use carefully-selected texts to do the following:

- Highlight the roles of author and illustrator.

- Identify the parts of a book.

- Introduce text types.

- Compare and contrast fiction and nonfiction.

- Ask thought-provoking questions.

If our goal for a read-aloud is to allow students to "focus their mental energy on the words and ideas presented in the text," then we have to carefully select books that will give them something to focus on.

Harness the power of read-alouds.

Why the Read-Aloud Is Essential in the Era of Higher Standards

The Read-Aloud:

❋ Fosters a strong sense of community.

❋ Builds a shared textual lineage, a wealth of reading experiences from which to draw when reading, writing, thinking, and talking about texts and when asked to *compare and contrast literary texts or informational texts about real-world situations.*

❋ Demonstrates how books work so that readers have a better understanding of *craft and structure.*

❋ Provides a catalyst for rich discussions and *collaborative conversations.*

❋ Models how proficient readers read *increasingly complex texts* by applying strategies, monitoring comprehension, and reading with fluency and expression.

❋ Offers children opportunities to recognize and identify how characters are feeling and acting, to acknowledge different perspectives, and to empathize with others, in order to better understand and express their own *feelings, perspectives, and opinions.*

❋ Helps all learners, especially English Language Learners, hear the *nuances of the English language* including intonation, pauses, rhythm, and pronunciation. In addition, listeners hear how the inflection of voice, tone, or phrasing can change *the meaning of words and phrases.*

(Adapted from Month-by-Month Reading Instruction for the Differentiated Classroom *[Walther & Phillips, 2012])*

Read-Alouds About the Power of Books and Reading

Elephant's Story (Pearson, 2013)	An elephant finds Gracie's lost book and sniffs the letters up his trunk. Elephant takes the mixed-up letters to all of his friends who are unable to put them back in order. Finally, Gracie returns, puts the words back in order, and shares the beginning of the story with her new friend, Elephant. This book is perfect for kindergarten!
The Fantastic Flying Books of Mr. Morris Lessmore (Joyce, 2012)	When Morris loses all of his books in a storm, he discovers an abandoned library alive with books. This story about the power of reading and writing will spark conversations and contains Tier 2 vocabulary to discuss, such as *mysterious, extraordinary,* and *weary.*
My Pet Book (Staake, 2014)	A boy in Smartytown selects a "frisky red hardcover" book for his pet.
Open This Little Book (Klausmeier, 2013)	The joys of reading one book after another are celebrated in this uniquely designed picture book.

DEVELOP TEXT SETS

During the school day, books are read aloud for different purposes. We read books for fun and to engage and entertain students. During reading workshop, carefully selected titles help demonstrate strategies used by skilled readers. We choose mentor texts for writing workshop to illuminate craft and structure decisions; for science or social studies lessons we might locate informational texts and digital media to build students' understanding of a certain topic. My colleagues and I have spent many years researching the best books for primary-grade readers and writers. The result of that work can be found in the following professional resources:

- *Literature Is Back!* (Fuhler & Walther, 2007)
- *Month-by-Month Trait-Based Writing Instruction* (Walther & Phillips, 2009)
- *Teaching Struggling Readers With Poetry* (Walther & Fuhler, 2010)
- *Month-by-Month Reading Instruction for the Differentiated Classroom* (Walther & Phillips, 2012)

I have learned to be strategic and purposeful when selecting my read-aloud titles. I believe this is the first step to elevating the read-aloud portion of reading workshop—selecting read-aloud texts with a purpose in mind. With the standards guiding our way, we can develop text sets to read during inquiry experiences across a week or during an instructional unit. The first type of text set to consider is a multi-genre text set.

Multi-Genre Text Sets

Multi-genre text sets promote thinking and discussion across texts and help learners integrate knowledge and ideas. You can put together multi-genre text sets to illuminate a theme or explore a particular topic. Then, when it's time to write about reading, invite students to apply their growing understanding by penning their own theme- or topic-related texts. For example, when exploring the theme of friendship, read a poem about friends, then a picture book about friendship, and follow that by writing a how-to piece about being a good friend. Here are a few multi-genre texts sets to get you started.

MULTI-GENRE TEXT SET—DANDELIONS

Poem: "Dandelion" found in *Come to My Party and Other Shape Poems* (Roemer, 2004, p. 21)

Narrative Picture Book: *The Dandelion's Tale* (Sheehan, 2014)

Informational Text(s): *A Dandelion's Life* (Himmelman, 1998); *From Seed to Dandelion* (Weiss, 2008)

MULTI-GENRE TEXT SET—SEEDS/PLANTS

Poem: "Maytime Magic" by Mabel Watts found in *The Random House Book of Poetry for Children* (Prelutsky, 1983, p. 44)

Narrative Picture Book: *Miss Maple's Seeds* (Wheeler, 2013)

Informational Text: *A Seed Is Sleepy* (Aston, 2007)

MULTI-GENRE TEXT SET—SLOTHS

Poem: "Slow Sloth's Slow Song" found in *Something Big Has Been Here* (Prelutsky, 1990, p. 65)

Narrative Picture Book: *Sparky!* (Offill, 2014)

Informational Text(s): *Let's Look at Sloths* (Piehl, 2011); *A Little Book of Sloth* (Cooke, 2013)

MULTI-GENRE TEXT SET—WORMS

Poem(s): "Heads or Tails" found in *Poetry Parade* (Vicker, 2006); "A Worm" found in *My Dog May Be a Genius* (Prelutsky, 2008)

Narrative Picture Book: *Superworm* (Donaldson, 2012)

Informational Text: *Earthworms* (Llewellyn, 2000)

Reading aloud multi-genre texts sets will help students discover connections between texts and broaden their background knowledge.

Multi-Level Text Sets

Multi-level text sets will help readers climb the ladder of complex texts. To assemble a multi-level text set, find a set of three to five texts about the same topic, concept, or theme. Read each text. Order them by complexity, even if they are the same guided-reading or lexile level (quantitative measures). Consider the following qualitative characteristics to help you determine the complexity of the text.

1. **Concepts**—As you read, think about your readers and their background knowledge.
   - Do readers have background knowledge or life experiences related to the theme, or are the themes abstract and the experiences depicted different from those of your students?

- Do readers have to make connections to other texts or to worldly events to understand the story? If so, this is a more complex text.
- Does the text include simple, everyday, concrete ideas or do learners need prior knowledge of the content to comprehend this text?

2. **Theme (Fiction)/Purpose (Nonfiction)**—While reading, notice how the author reveals the theme/central message/moral or the purpose for writing the informational text.
   - Is the theme clear and revealed early in the text, or do readers have to infer the theme based on reading the entire text?
   - Does the author clearly state a narrowly focused purpose, or do readers have to infer a more abstract purpose?

3. **Vocabulary/Language**—When reading the text, notice the complexity of the language, the sentence structures, and the vocabulary words you might need to define.
   - Is the language literal, straightforward, and easy to understand, or will readers have to have knowledge of abstract, figurative language?
   - Are the sentences simple or complex?
   - Is the vocabulary up-to-date, familiar, and conversational, or unfamiliar, old-fashioned, academic, or otherwise complex? How many words would you have to help your listeners define?

4. **Text Structure/Length**—Think about the number of narrative events or the amount of information students will have to keep track of as they listen.
   - Does the narrative text have multiple characters or storylines? If so, it is probably a bit more complex than a text with a single storyline.
   - Does the informational text make connections between a number of different events or pieces of information? Again, if so, this text would be more complex.

Once the texts are ordered by complexity, read them aloud and provide the scaffolding and support necessary for your students to understand each text as they grow more complex. As you get to the longer texts with more complex structures, read them as you would a chapter book, over a number of days, allowing plenty of time for collaborative conversations to boost comprehension.

INCORPORATE INFORMATIONAL TEXTS

When looking for ways to incorporate informational texts into read-aloud fare, pairing fiction with nonfiction titles simply makes sense. Reading aloud a fiction title will often lead students to ask questions that are quickly answered by doing a little research using multimedia resources or informational texts. Having paired fiction-and-nonfiction sets at your fingertips makes this a bit easier. By reading aloud nonfiction books, we are balancing the types of books we read to children (Fuhler & Walther, 2007). For a teaching routine using a list of paired fiction and informational texts, see page 88. Along with pairing texts, simply making a point to balance your read-alouds across the week is another way to infuse informational text. Since I know that I tend to read aloud more fiction than nonfiction, I've been on a quest for engaging, well-written informational read-alouds. You'll find a few of my favorites on page 49 and others in Part 2.

A Few of My Favorite Informational Read-Alouds

Eat Like a Bear (Sayre, 2013)	Follow a brown bear from April, when she wakes up from hibernation, until November, when she hibernates again.	EAT LIKE A BEAR APRIL PULLEY SAYRE *Illustrated by* STEVE JENKINS
How Big Were Dinosaurs? (Judge, 2013)	Illuminate the nonfiction writing technique of comparison as your students learn about dinosaurs from the tiniest to the largest.	
Lizards (Bishop, 2010)	Select any of Nic Bishop's captivating nonfiction titles to share with your students. I read his books aloud like I would a chapter book, highlighting one or two pages each day providing time to notice how Bishop's stunning photographs help describe the key ideas.	
Surprising Sharks (Davies, 2005)	Readers learn that sharks come in many shapes and sizes and that most are not dangerous. Compare and contrast this book with Tedd Arnold's *Fly Guy Presents: Sharks* (2013).	

PROVIDE LOTS OF SUPPORT

I've suggested a few ways to increase the complexity of the texts students are hearing during reading workshop. My experience teaching young learners for almost three decades tells me that we have to intentionally facilitate successful experiences with such texts or we will leave many of our students behind. To support students as they read complex texts, Elfrieda Hiebert (2012) suggests the following six actions:

1. **Focus on building learners' knowledge.** In addition to building students' knowledge of content-area concepts, it is essential that we focus on the insights learners gain from reading literary texts. For primary-grade children, this means helping readers uncover the themes found in the literature we read aloud. To do this, select texts that illuminate themes such as accepting differences, working together, or being courageous. For an inquiry experience and sample texts to help students uncover themes, see page 114.

2. **Guide readers in discovering connections.** When reading a text, you can help your students discover connections in a number of different ways.

   - Connect learners' existing schema to the content contained in the new text by quickly asking them what they already think they know about the topic.

   - Set a purpose for reading that highlights the new learning gained from reading the text, saying something like, "Today we're going to add to your schema about [topic] and learn more about [a certain aspect of that topic]."

   - Show students how to combine their new learning with their existing schema using graphic organizers or by writing about their reading.

   - Gather additional electronic media sources to widen students' knowledge about the topic.

   - Provide opportunities for students to share and discuss their new learning with others.

3. **Activate readers' engagement.** To foster engagement, provide choice in what students read and an opportunity to read widely and deeply about a variety of topics. When you find topics that interest your students, gather books on those topics at increasing levels of complexity. That way you can keep them engaged while, at the same time, supporting them as they inch toward reading more complex texts.

4. **Expand learners' vocabulary.** In addition to the proven power of read-alouds to build students' vocabulary, helping your students develop strategies for clarifying the meaning of unknown words along with teaching them about word relationships is key to expanding their vocabulary. You'll find teaching routines and inquiry experiences for both in Part 2. When students can independently employ these strategies, they will be better able to tackle complex texts.

5. **Increase the volume.** For years, I've been asking, "Why do we make thing so complicated?" Primary-grade students need teachers who know books, have a lot of books, can match books to readers, and can give them time to read, read, read. In fact, "An additional 7 minutes of reading per day has been found to be the difference in classrooms where students read well from those were students read less well" (Hiebert, 2012, p. 6). Think about it. Are your most struggling students independently reading for at least seven minutes each day? If not, what can you do to inch up their time? At the beginning of the year, that may mean sitting with a small group of emergent readers and showing them how to read one book after another.

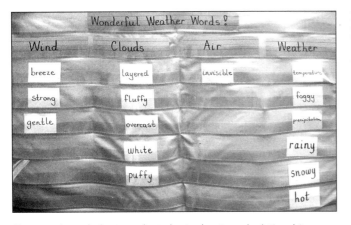

To expand vocabulary, teach students about word relationships.

6. **Build reading stamina.** In order to increase the volume students are reading, we have to help them to build their stamina to focus and read independently. If they are going to be expected to read complex texts, think critically across extended texts, and compare and contrast texts, they have to be able to read for a long time. Increasing the volume of reading and boosting students' reading stamina are key features of a successful reading workshop.

You've learned a few tips for selecting read-aloud texts. Now, let's discuss how to elevate the read-aloud experience with comprehension conversations.

Collaborative Conversations

Collaborative Conversations → *Collaborative conversations initiated by students in response to peers' questions, thoughts, and opinions permeate the day.*

You've probably had the experience of opening the teacher's manual of a packaged reading program to find endless questions to ask readers or listeners about a piece of text. Rarely do those same manuals invite readers or listeners to pose their own questions or collaborate to build knowledge. Shifting this responsibility away from the teacher as "questioner" or "discussion leader" is the next way to elevate your workshop. We want to teach our students how to ask and answer questions and build knowledge by collaborating with their classmates. In Chapter 6, there are two inquiry experiences that will guide you in supporting students as they learn to pose questions and collaborate. As I tell my first graders, "Every time you listen to someone else's thinking, you get smarter!" Collaborative conversations that surround read-aloud experiences are essential to helping children develop the habits of mind we learned about earlier. The standards document echoes this belief and says, "Children in the early grades—particularly kindergarten through grade 3—benefit from participating in rich, structured conversations with an adult in response to written texts that are read aloud, orally and comparing and contrasting as well as analyzing and synthesizing" (CCSS, p. 27). These rich, structured conversations or "comprehension conversations" are "an interactive discussion about a piece of text that is best sparked by posing higher-level questions and inviting students to listen to and respond to their peers' thoughts and ideas" (Walther & Phillips, 2012, p. 21). Certainly, productive conversations don't magically happen overnight. They do happen when you support students by helping them develop the conversational norms and types of language and questions that move a conversation forward. I'll share these specific learning experiences that scaffold students as they develop their conversation skills on pages 102–105.

For many young learners who are not yet able to put their thoughts in written words, their reading responses will take the form of conversations. Eventually, bolstered by the practice of frequent comprehension conversations, they will be able to respond to their reading in illustrations or writing.

Reading Response

> **Reading Response** → *Reading responses are based on prior knowledge and experience coupled with text-based evidence.*

Tips for Reading Response

※ Build on evidence-based conversations.

※ Ask "big" questions.

※ Identify the audience and purpose.

※ Demonstrate high-quality responses.

※ Develop shared criteria.

※ Provide descriptive feedback.

Think back to the evidence-based conversations you read about in Chapter 1 (pp. 17–18). Conversations like these lay the groundwork for evidence-based reading responses. Young children need a lot of practice zooming in on the text and illustrations to locate evidence and then articulating their discoveries orally and in written words or pictures. Because reading and writing are reciprocal processes, this type of thinking supports children not only as writers, but also as readers. The standards emphasize the importance of students writing about the information they find in text and illustrations because this research-supported practice increases learners' reading comprehension (IRA CCSS Committee, 2012). Just as the evidence-based discussions revolve around higher-level or "big" questions, so too should students' reading responses. You know as well as I do that the act of writing extended pieces of text is challenging for young learners. So instead of asking students to respond to a series of questions, consider asking one big question that will help encapsulate their understanding of the text. A sampling of big questions is provided on pages 52–53. As with any type of writing, children will gain a better understanding of how to craft an effective response if they can watch you do it first. Then, based on this experience, work with students to develop a shared criteria so that they can self-assess their own response. Finally, as students are writing, walk around to provide on-the-spot descriptive feedback to improve their pieces. To supplement the ideas found in Chapter 5, you will find a wealth of reading response ideas in *Month-by-Month Reading Instruction for the Differentiated Classroom* (Walther & Phillips, 2012).

A Sampling of "Big" Questions

Book	Summary	"Big" Question	Sample Response
Fireflies (Brinckloe, 1985) GRL: K	A boy and his friends catch hundreds of fireflies in jars. Then he learns that sometimes you need to set something free in order to keep it.	What would you have done with the fireflies? Why?	"I would use a tank so they have more room."
Freedom on the Menu: The Greensboro Sit-Ins (Weatherford, 2005) GRL: M	Set in 1960, this picture book tells the story of the civil rights sit-ins from the perspective of eight-year-old Connie, who is unable to sit at the lunch counter at Woolworth's for a banana split.	Why do you think it was the best banana split Connie ever had?	2/22 Freedom on the Menu. Why do you think It was the best banana split Connie ever had? Because it was on the day that... She got to eat it on the counter. I also notest that she ate it next to her brother and sister boo helpt make it posibel. *Because it was on the day that... she got to eat at the counter. I also noticed that she ate it next to her brother and sister who helped make it possible.*
Grandfather Twilight (Berger, 1984)	This is the story of how Grandfather Twilight puts the world to sleep at night.	Can you think of a different title for this story? Use evidence from the text to explain why.	Getting Darker (with every magical step) Why? Because Grandfather twilight used his magic to make day into night. He walked in the forest until his pearl was the moon.

Book	Summary	"Big" Question	Sample Response
How Many Days to America? (Bunting, 1988) GRL: S	The American ideals of freedom and safety are highlighted in Bunting's tale of a Caribbean family that flees on a small, crowded fishing boat to America.	How is this story the same as or different than the Pilgrims' story? How is it different?	They are both people. They both came to America by boat. They both came to America because they hope to have a better life for their family. They both celebrate Thanksgiving for the first time in America. The Pilgrims have taller hats. Both groups got freedom in America.
The Magic Fish (Littledale, 1966) GRL: L	The Magic Fish grants a greedy fisherman's wife every wish but she still isn't satisfied.	What words would you use to describe the wife? Use ideas from the book to support your thinking.	Bossy- She is giving orders. Ungrateful- She is not thankful for what she has. Selfish- She dose not care about the fisherman. Greedy. She wants everything.
Too Many Tamales (Soto, 1993) GRL: M	While helping to make tamales, Maria, a young Latina child, puts on her mother's wedding ring then forgets about it. Later, when it is time to eat the tamales she realizes the ring is lost. Will Maria find the ring?	I think a different title for this book might be _____ because . . . Use ideas from the book to support your thinking.	I think a different title for this book might be "Should we eat all the tamales?" because I want the readers to think if telling the truth is easier than covering up the problem.

(Levels listed are Fountas & Pinnell [2009] Guided Reading Levels.)

Mini-Lessons

> **Mini-Lessons** → *A series of mini-lessons is centered on big ideas integrated across language arts strands (reading, writing, speaking, listening, viewing/visually representing).*

Mini-lessons are, and always will be, a vital component of the workshop. It is a consistent time to explicitly showcase specific aspects of literacy instruction. During the reading workshop, mini-lessons usually focus on the following aspects:

- Inspiring and motivating readers

- Comprehension strategies

- Foundational skills: word recognition and fluency

- Language standards: grammar and vocabulary

- Genre awareness

You will find standards-based learning experiences that match each of these aspects in Chapter 5. A way to transform instruction during mini-lessons is to take a wide-angle view of the lessons. Instead of planning each mini-lesson as a separate entity, consider the end goal or big idea that you want your students to be able to do and know. Using the standards, which are written as end-of-year goals, you can design a series of mini-lessons to teach the prerequisite skills, strategies, and habits of mind to reach a particular destination.

Sample Mini-Lesson Series

End Goal/Big Idea: Identify basic similarities and differences between two texts on the same topic.

Preparation	Mini-Lesson 1	Mini-Lesson 2	Mini-Lesson 3	Mini-Lesson 4	Mini-Lesson 5
Carefully select straightforward examples of two diverse informational texts on the same topic.	Introduce the topic and the terms *similar/different* or *compare/contrast*. Share, discuss, and chart noticings from the first text.	Share, discuss, and chart noticings from the second text.	Compare and contrast the two texts. Notice and discuss how and why the authors chose the two different approaches.	Apply discoveries to another pair of texts.	Invite students to try something they discovered in their own writing. Share and celebrate writers' experimentation and approximations.

EMBEDDED COMPREHENSION STRATEGY INSTRUCTION

Comprehension Strategies → *Overarching themes and big ideas as the organizing feature: comprehension strategies are used as tools to better understand text.*

As more and more individuals in and out of the field of education write about implementing the standards, there are misconceptions that are being touted as the "new Common Core way" to teach readers. I believe this occurs because people are still looking for the "one right way" to teach when, time and time again, research has shown that it is *the knowledgeable teacher* who makes the difference (International Reading Association, 2000). As professionals, we have to make sure that common sense and research-based, dynamic teaching practices prevail. One misconception I've heard is that there is no longer a place for reading-strategy instruction because the strategies are not explicitly outlined in the standards document. Anyone who has worked with young readers knows this is ridiculous, and many experts agree—including long-standing comprehension researchers like Ellin Keene and Susan Zimmerman, who remind us that strategies are tools that lead students to become proficient, avid readers (Keene & Zimmerman, 2013). This sentiment is echoed in the International Reading Association's document *Literacy Implementation Guidance for the ELA Common Core State Standards*, which states, "Given the extensive body of high-quality research conducted into the effectiveness and benefits of explicit comprehension strategy instruction, teachers should also rededicate themselves to teaching such strategies in the future as another avenue to accomplish the Core Standards" (IRA CCSS Committee, 2012, p. 2). Of course, as Keene and Zimmerman point out, *"The strategies are a means to an end, not an end in themselves"* (2013, p. 605, italics theirs). Their words serve as a reminder that we are not teaching "predicting"; rather we are helping children understand how the metacognitive process of predicting, or thinking ahead of their reading, helps to better engage them in the act of reading and, as a result, gain deeper understanding of the text. If we approach comprehension strategy instruction with that mindset, our mini-lessons will be much richer.

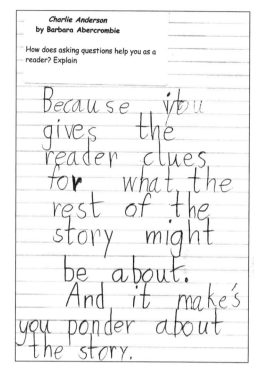

Ask students how the comprehension strategies help them as readers.

FOUNDATIONAL SKILLS INSTRUCTION: WORD RECOGNITION AND FLUENCY

Foundational skills encompass these four skill areas:

- **Print Concepts:** Development of learners' knowledge of basic print concepts along with letter recognition in kindergarten

- **Phonological Awareness:** Development of students' understanding of spoken words, syllables, and sounds

- **Phonics and Word Recognition:** Instruction in decoding strategies, high-frequency words, and word analysis

- **Fluency:** Instruction in self-monitoring strategies and fluency (accuracy, rate, and expression)

Celebrate early writers' attempts to use their own developmental spelling.

When I work with teachers and school districts implementing the standards, the foundational skills strand seems to be the one that provides the biggest challenge. Schools are often looking for a one-size-fits-all packaged program that will teach all of these skills when we've known for decades that a knowledgeable teacher armed with dynamic teaching practices is what's truly effective. The CCSS recognizes this fact: "Instruction [in foundational skills] should be differentiated: good readers will need much less practice with these concepts than struggling readers will. The point is to teach students what they need to learn and not what they already know—to discern when particular children or activities warrant more or less attention" (CCSS, p. 15). For example, when it comes to developing phonemic awareness, one of the best ways for youngsters to apply their growing knowledge of spoken sounds is simply to write. Studies have shown that kindergarten teachers who promote early writing activities by encouraging learners to use developmental spelling and by demonstrating how to sound-stretch while they compose morning messages or engage in interactive writing lessons see a growth in students' ability to segment phonemes (McGill-Franzen, Allington, Yokoi, & Brooks, 1999; Scanlon & Vellutino, 1997). *This means we should celebrate early writers' attempts to use their own developmental spelling rather than expecting that every word children write will be spelled conventionally.* In addition to daily writing, your phonemic-awareness instruction should consist of developmentally appropriate activities that are engaging, interactive, social, and that develop students' curiosity about and desire to experiment with the sounds of language (Yopp, 1992). We can use dynamic teaching practices such as interactive reading to highlight print concepts (see teaching routine below), phonetic elements, and sight words, and also to strengthen fluency.

Using Interactive Reading to Teach Print Concepts

TARGETS

- I can show you how books work.
- I can show you how words work.
- I can show you how sentences work.

PREPARATION

When selecting text for interactive reading, choose text large enough for all of your students to see and low enough for them to be able to touch, write on, or point to. This ensures that they can interact with the text as you refer to particular word families, highlight sight words, or reread to build fluency. The following materials work well for interactive read-aloud:

- Picture books
- Big books
- Pocket charts
- An overhead, document camera, or interactive whiteboard
- Poetry
- Songs and song picture books
- Pointers of various shapes and sizes

EXPLANATION

The overarching aim of interactive reading is to teach readers how spoken language is represented by printed text; that's why it's an ideal teaching routine for building students' foundational skills. The interactive reading experience here is focused on print concepts. As you read and enjoy the text, invite students to notice and demonstrate their understanding of left-to-right voice-print match, directional rules such as where we begin reading and how to do a return sweep (move from the end of one line to the beginning of the next), the concept of a word, spaces between words—and eventually in Grade 1, the features of a sentence.

A Few of My Favorite Song Picture Books

Octopus's Garden (Starr, 2014)	If you're a Beatles fan, then you need to add this song picture book to your collection! Illustrator Ben Cort takes you on a on a magical journey through the Octopus's Garden. Includes CD recording of the song (not the Beatles' version!).
Sing (Raposo & Lichtenheld, 2013)	If you watched Sesame Street as a young child, you might remember the song "Sing." This song of courage, pride, and hope comes to life with Tom Lichtenheld's brilliant illustrations. The picture book also includes a CD so that your class can sing along.
Take Me Home, Country Roads (Denver, 2005)	After the hectic backpack packing, we end our day together singing this song. Canyon's quilt-like illustrations bring this song to life for a whole new generation.
There Was an Old Monster! (Emberley, Emberley, & Emberley, 2009)	A new twist on the cumulative rhyme, "There Was an Old Lady Who Swallowed a Fly." In this version, when the old monster swallowed some ants, "man those ants had him dancing in his pants. Scritchy-scratch, Scritch, scritchy, scratch!" Download the song—it's a blast!

EXPERIENCE

While reading an enlarged text, explicitly point out the concepts of print by asking the questions below and inviting children to join you and interact with the printed text.

- Place a big book on the easel upside down with back of book facing the students. Ask, "Can someone find the front of this book?" "What clues helped you to know that it was the front?" (orientation of book)

- Pause on a page of text with illustrations. Ask, "Where should I begin reading?" How do you know that?" (Concept that print, not illustrations carry the written message)

- Display a page with multiple lines of text. Say, "Show me where I should begin reading. Which way do I go when I read?" At the end of a line wonder, "Where do I read after that?" (directional rules)

- As you are reading, use a pointer to track individual words. Ask students to do the same. (one-to-one match)

- Select a page with only one sentence on it. Ask learners to point to the first word in the sentence, and then to the last word in the sentence. Ask, "Why is the first letter of the first word different from the others?" (concept of sentence)

- Highlight and discuss the purpose of various punctuation marks.

- To further this learning experience, place the same materials in the reading center so that students can teach each other as they reread favorite texts. In addition, you can engage in book-related discussions with your students during small-group guided-reading lessons. For further suggestions for Pre-A Guided Reading, see Jan Richardson's book *The Next Step in Guided Reading* (2009). Confer with students and ask the same questions that you did in the learning experience to assess whether they've mastered the concepts of print. For a more formal measure of print concepts you can administer either *Next Step Guided Reading Assessment K–2, Pre-A Assessment* (Richardson & Walther, 2013) or *Concepts About Print Observation Task* (Clay, 2000).

LANGUAGE INSTRUCTION: GRAMMAR AND VOCABULARY

Instruction in how language works is comprised of two main areas:

- **Grammar:** Teaching the grammar and usage needed to be an effective writer and speaker and the conventions that strong writers employ, including spelling

- **Vocabulary Acquisition and Use:** Instruction in determining the meaning of words, understanding word relationships and the nuances of words, and using learned words and phrases

With these two areas in mind, it is easy to see where to focus on these skills and strategies. Obviously, when you're teaching the conventions of standard English and spelling, the majority of that instruction will take place during the writing workshop and word-study lessons so that children have immediate opportunities to apply their understanding. Therefore, I will talk more about this area in Chapter 4. Effective vocabulary instruction is woven into both workshops; since the focus of this chapter is reading workshop, let's take a moment to review the tenets of research-based, embedded vocabulary instruction. You will find specific vocabulary-related teaching routines and inquiry experiences in Chapters 5 and 6.

Long before the CCSS arrived at our classroom doors, we've known the importance of creating instructional experiences that build young children's vocabulary knowledge, especially for those students from low socioeconomic backgrounds, English language learners, and struggling readers. "Research shows that the explicit teaching of the meanings of such words and parts of words, along with reading to students and encouraging them to engage in their own extensive reading, can steadily build such vocabulary knowledge." (IRA CCSS Committee, 2012, p. 3). This, once again, underscores the importance of read-aloud and independent reading as non-negotiable components of a reading workshop.

Guiding Readers

Guiding Readers → *Teachers guide readers in many different ways. In small groups, the instructional focus and content of guided-reading lessons changes based on students' level of reading development and, if needed, includes word study and guided writing.*

The components of the workshop are designed to reflect the successful, research-based gradual release of responsibility model of teaching. During mini-lessons, teachers model the use of a strategy, and then guide readers to apply that strategy while coaching them individually or in small groups. As students progress, we gradually reduce the amount of scaffolding and support so that during independent reading students are able to integrate that strategy, along with others they've learned, to increase their comprehension (IRA CCSS Committee, 2012). When we guide readers, we say to them, "Let's try this together. I'm here to help!" So whether you choose to guide readers individually as you confer with them or in small groups while teaching targeted guided-reading lessons, your focus is on reinforcing a problem-solving action (Richardson, 2009). Meeting with students individually or in small groups allows you to "tailor your whole-class instruction so that you move the majority of your students in a way that has real traction, and then tailor small-group teaching to support students who are earlier or more advanced in their level of skill development" (Calkins, Ehrenworth, & Lehman, 2012, p. 53). The ultimate goal of all this work is for children to apply what they've learned from your mini-lessons and targeted coaching during conferences or guided reading while independently reading just-right books.

NEXT STEP GUIDED READING

Professional books and collegial conversations are so helpful when ramping up your guided reading instruction. If you haven't read Jan Richardson's book *The Next Step in Guided Reading* (2009), I highly recommend that you add it to your "someday" professional book list. Jan's book helped me understand how the teaching focus of guided-reading lessons evolves as children progress through the stages of reading development from emergent readers to fluent readers. (See the chart below.) In addition, she clearly lays out a three-pronged approach to teaching guided reading that includes word study and guided writing. Engaging in ongoing professional conversations as you implement guided reading is the key to making changes in your instruction. For now, I'll give you a quick overview of the three steps to preparing to teach an effective Next Step Guided Reading lesson (Richardson & Walther, 2013).

The Three Steps to Effective Next Step Guided Reading Lessons

1. Analyze data from the running record to pinpoint an instructional focus.

2. Select an instructional-level text to match your teaching focus.

3. Determine teaching points and scaffold readers so they can take the next step in becoming more independent.

Step 1: Analyze Data to Pinpoint an Instructional Focus

Emergent Readers	Early Readers	Transitional Readers	Fluent Readers
CONCEPT OF A WORD DECODING STRATEGIES • Picture clues • Beginning-sound clues • Cross-checking/ self-monitoring SIGHT WORDS COMPREHENSION • Retelling • Building background • Making predictions • Making connections • Noticing text patterns	DECODING STRATEGIES • Rereading • Using context clues • Looking for chunks • Self-monitoring SIGHT WORDS FLUENCY VOCABULARY RETELLING COMPREHENSION CONVERSATIONS • Comparing/ contrasting texts • Inferring big ideas • Stating/defending opinions	INTEGRATING DECODING STRATEGIES SELF-MONITORING WORD ANALYSIS FLUENCY VOCABULARY RETELLING COMPREHENSION CONVERSATIONS • Comparing/ contrasting texts • Inferring big ideas • Stating/defending opinions	SELF-MONITORING WITH AUTOMATICITY WORD ANALYSIS FLUENCY VOCABULARY RETURNING TO TEXT/ TEXT-BASED EVIDENCE COMPREHENSION CONVERSATIONS • Reading critically • Discussing plot and purposes of different text structures • Discussing various interpretations of text

Step 2: Select an Instructional-Level Text to Match Your Teaching Focus

- **Self-monitoring**—Does the book have a clear illustration-to-text match?

- **Decoding**—Does the text contain known sight words along with those that might pose a decoding challenge, such as multisyllabic words, words with specific endings, and so on?

- **Fluency**—Does the story include dialogue?

- **Vocabulary**— Does the book include vocabulary or concepts that are easily defined using context clues, visual cues, or the glossary?

- **Comprehension**—Does the character change over time? Does the book lend itself to a discussion of its lesson or moral?

Step 3: Determine Teaching Points and Scaffold Readers

- **Monitoring**—First and foremost, if the reader is not monitoring for meaning, we scaffold, prompt, and teach this foundational skill. Fostering a child's ability to self-monitor and self-correct is key!

- **Decoding**—If the reader stops at a tricky word, then we prompt for decoding strategies and reinforce decoding as a teaching point.

- **Fluency**—Fluency comes next because once a reader develops automaticity with words and decoding, he or she is ready to be prompted for fluency.

- **Vocabulary**—It is common for skilled decoders to plow right through unknown words, decode them accurately, but not use the context clues to figure out the meaning of the word. Scaffolding vocabulary is an ideal teaching point for transitional and fluent readers!

- **Comprehension**—Comprehension appears last in the sequence because it is the *goal of every guided-reading lesson* and the previous scaffolds and teaching points will support the readers' understanding of the text.

With a bit of modification, the three steps can be applied to independent reading and conferring. The major difference is that, with your guidance, students choose their own texts for independent reading and those texts *must* be high-success texts (see pages 100–101 for a description of high-success texts).

"Independent" Reading

Independent Reading → *Surround "independent" reading by actively structuring conditions, such as explicit instruction and teacher monitoring, to increase students' accountability and progress toward reading more complex texts.*

You'll notice the word "independent" is in quotation marks. The reason for that is twofold. First, when you teach young learners, it takes a lot of modeling and support to help them independently engage in any activity. Second, independent reading is only as successful as the conditions that surround it (see box on page 61), the most important one being a teacher who is actively "structuring, guiding, teaching, interacting with, monitoring, and holding students accountable for time spent reading" (Reutzel, Jones, & Newman, 2010, p. 176).

Transforming Literacy Teaching in the Era of Higher Standards, K–2 © 2015 by Maria P. Walther, Scholastic Teaching Resources

As you can see, the conditions that support independent reading parallel those that surround the workshop. In addition, the steps you take to prepare for independent reading are similar to those I previously shared for guided reading.

The Three Steps to Effective Independent Reading

1. Guide students in selecting just-right texts that match their interests and independent reading ability.

2. When conferring, use data from analyzing the running record or from listening to the student read to pinpoint a brief instructional focus.

3. Determine which teaching points will scaffold readers so they can take the next step in becoming more independent. Remember that the type of text he or she is reading should influence the specific strategies you encourage the student to use (Miller & Moss, 2013).

Each day, during independent reading, take a moment to look up from your conference or guided-reading group. As you look around, notice which children are engaged and which are not. Jot down the names of the disengaged children so that you can bring them together to check that they have just-right books or discuss strategies for building their stamina. This check-in is essential to ensuring that students are using their independent reading time wisely. As with all aspects of reading workshop, independent reading flourishes with an intentional focus on classroom culture and the continued monitoring of students' progress by conferring with readers on a regular basis.

> ## Critical Classroom Conditions for Effective Independent Reading
>
> ❋ **Time**—Daily in-class time to read
>
> ❋ **Choice**—Student-selected texts
>
> ❋ **Explicit Instruction**—Mini-lessons and demonstrations on what, why, and how readers read
>
> ❋ **Volume and Variety**—Gaining experience by reading a wide variety of genres
>
> ❋ **Access**—Well-stocked classroom libraries
>
> ❋ **Teacher Monitoring**—Brief, teacher-initiated, individual student conferences
>
> ❋ **Collaborative Conversations**—Small-group text discussions to enhance higher-level thinking, metacognitive strategy use, and the ability to structure arguments
>
> *(Miller & Moss, 2013, p. 16)*

CONFERRING

Conferring with readers is an essential element of the reading workshop. It is a time to sit down one-on-one with each child and discover what he or she needs in order to continue to build stamina and progress as a reader. I'll admit, it isn't always easy to carve out time to confer, and I'm constantly refining the management of an effective reading conference, but when I see the difference it makes in the life of a reader, I know it is well worth the effort!

In his book, *Conferring: The Keystone of a Reader's Workshop* (2009, p. 34), Patrick Allen shares the reasons he confers:

- Uncover readers' attitudes toward reading and how they see themselves as readers.

- Discover learners' stamina and work ethic by noticing how they manage their reading life.

- Explore readers' processes.

- Record readers' preferences by asking what they are reading and why.

- Form a relationship of intimacy and rigor by discovering how readers interact with texts.

- Gather data for ongoing assessment by asking students to describe what they know and are able to do.

Types of Reading Conferences

To streamline and focus the reading conference, my colleagues Karen and Brian have created four types of conferences that they have with their students. I'll outline each here.

THE SHARING AND CELEBRATING CONFERENCE

Purpose: To build a relationship with the student, share a love of books, and celebrate growth

Possible Teaching Actions

- Ask, "What books do you have in your book box? Can you tell me how and why you chose them?"

- Say, "Catch me up!" "Tell me about what you've been reading today."

- Listen as the child shares what he or she has read.

- Jot down what you've noticed and learned about the child as a reader and possible next steps.

THE ASSESSMENT CONFERENCE

Purpose: To collect data from students that informs instruction and helps determine next instructional steps

Possible Teaching Actions

- Administer a formal reading assessment like the *Next Step Guided Reading Assessment, Grades K–2* (Richardson & Walther, 2013).

- Use informal formative assessment or anecdotal observations to determine whether the child can apply a skill or strategy taught during an inquiry experience.

- Administer a running record as student reads from his or her self-selected book.

- Inquire about the child's reading preferences or at-home reading habits.

- Jot down what you've noticed and learned about the child as a reader and possible next steps.

THE TEACHING CONFERENCE

Purpose: To follow up on information gained from an assessment conference or observations made during whole-class or small-group instruction

Possible Teaching Actions

- Demonstrate how to use a specific skill or strategy.

- Use questions, prompts, and cues to guide a student as he or she applies a specific skill or strategy.

- Help students recognize how particular texts are organized and how that structure can support them as readers.

- Work with students to plan for reading a variety of genres, authors, and texts with increasing levels of difficulty. Encourage them to read books that give them something to think about (Miller & Moss, 2013).

- Jot down skill or strategy taught.

Oftentimes, you will notice a reader engaging in a behavior or strategy that you want to call attention to in order to benefit others in the class. When this happens, invite that child to share it with the class during sharing and celebration time at the end of reading workshop.

Sharing and Celebrating

Sharing and Celebrating → *Sharing and celebration are focused on reflections about how readers went about learning—the process or strategies that were independently applied.*

During workshop sharing, children articulate the learning that occurred while reading independently, learning alongside their peers, or conferring with the teacher. Youngsters are excited to share their discoveries with their peers, and there are some who would love to share every day! To make sharing time more focused and purposeful, I usually encourage children whom I've conferred or met with to share their insights first, and then open it up to the rest of the class. From Debbie Miller (2013a), I learned the "big" question that drives the sharing: "What did you learn about yourself as a reader today?" This is followed by, "Can you teach that to your friends?" Sharing brings closure to the workshop, strengthens the sense of community, and provides time to celebrate the small learning moments that occur every day.

Looking Back, Moving Forward

When you center your teaching on the core conditions of time, materials, choice, structure, and mentor or expert support, you create an engaging workshop environment where each day students are able to try and apply what they've learned. Along the way, they build stamina and understand the purpose of reading, speaking, listening, and thinking. Young children who are "raised" in such conditions are sure to become master craftspeople, able to make meaning out of letters and words.

Chapter 4

Enhancing Writing Workshop

Teaching Writing Is (Still) Challenging

Go online to view a video on Writing Workshop in Action; see page 160.

It has been six years since Katherine Phillips and I wrote *Month-by-Month Trait-Based Writing Instruction* (2009). You would think that after writing a book about writing workshop, traveling around the country talking about writing instruction, and teaching writing to my first graders each day, I would have it all figured out. Well, I don't! Teaching writing is still the most challenging part of my day, but it is also the most rewarding. I love welcoming reluctant writers—the ones with a severe dislike of anything involving a pencil or crayons—into the "writing club." I know I've made headway when those same children ask, "Can I work on my little books when I'm done with this?" Let's take a look at what I've learned about writing workshop since 2009 and how the more rigorous standards have enhanced my instructional practices.

Workshop Conditions

In Chapter 2, I highlighted the reciprocal processes of reading and writing and how my thinking about those processes has evolved over the years. In this chapter, although the focus is shifting from reading workshop to writing workshop, you'll notice the conditions are exactly the same. Think about the message that this sends to literacy learners and how it not only supports the goal of streamlining instruction, but also nudges students toward becoming self-directed, independent learners. We'll begin this chapter as we did the chapter on reading workshop by reviewing the workshop conditions beginning with the condition that poses the greatest challenge for all teachers, including myself—time.

Time

Although Writing Anchor Standard 10 does not appear in the CCSS until grade 3, I believe it provides direction for primary-grade teachers. We want students to "write routinely" so that they gain an understanding of how writers think, act, and work. Additionally, young children who consistently have time to write build their stamina. Whether they are working on a short piece or an extended project that may take a few weeks to complete, children learning in workshop classrooms know they will regularly have *time* to write. They do not spend valuable writing time copying the teacher's words from the board, filling in blanks on worksheets, completing a frame sentence by writing one word, or creating graphic organizers before they write. All of this "fake" writing wastes precious time and is not going to help children learn about the nuances of craft and structure in order to make intentional "writerly" decisions. Starting in kindergarten, children need frequent writing experiences so that they can learn how to adjust their communication based on audience, task, purpose, and content. If we, as teachers, are always making these decisions for young writers, they will never become independent learners. The National Commission on Writing echoes this belief saying, "If students are to make knowledge their own, they must struggle with the details, wrestle with the facts, and rework raw information and dimly understood concepts into language they can communicate to someone else. In short, if students are to learn, they must write" (2003, p. 9).

Materials

In 2009, we were just beginning to discover the power of "little books" as one of the main materials our writers use during what we call "student choice" writing time (Walther & Phillips, 2009, p. 26). In Katie Wood Ray and Lisa Cleaveland's book *About the Authors: Writing Workshop With Our Youngest Writers* (2004), I read about Lisa's students, who spend their writing workshop time making books. This brilliant idea transformed my writing workshop, and the more time I spend observing students as they compose little

Give students plenty of time to write.

Sample K–2 Writing Workshop Schedule *(30-60 minutes)*

READ LIKE A WRITER *5-10 min*

- Notice and name craft techniques in literary and informational texts.

- Develop an understanding of a specific genre.

- Analyze and evaluate written work.

MINI-LESSON: DEMONSTRATION/ SHARED DEMONSTRATION *5-10 min*

- Show or discuss how to apply what children have learned from reading like a writer.

- Model and think aloud while writing, or work with students on a shared piece.

GUIDED-WRITING TIME *5-30 min*

- Children write or are engaged in meaningful writing-related tasks (rereading, revising, peer editing, polishing, illustrating).

- Confer with individuals or meet with small guided-writing groups.

SHARING AND CELEBRATING *5-10 min*

- Students engage in whole-group share, in partner sharing, or in small authors' circle groups.

(From Month-by-Month Trait-Based Writing Instruction *[Walther & Phillips, 2009, p. 27])*

Observe young writers as they create their own little books.

How Do Little Books Help Young Writers?

Beginning writers who make books . . .

❋ Experience what it is like to live with an idea for a while.

❋ Make the "read like a writer" connection.

❋ Build an understanding of genre, audience, and purpose.

❋ Develop stamina for writing.

❋ Enhance their understanding of composition and decision making.

(Ray & Cleaveland, 2004)

Tips for Making and Managing Little Books

❋ Make an assortment of "little books" (blank paper) in various sizes and with varying number of pages.

- 5 ½- x 8 ½-inch (½ sheet of copy paper portrait, staple some on top and some on side)
- 4 ½- x 11-inch (½ sheet of copy paper landscape, staple some on top and some on side)
- 4 ¼- x 5 ½-inch (½ sheet of copy paper)

❋ Begin by giving students one to five "little books" with four pages each. If you find that kids are consistently filling four-page books, then move on to books that contain more pages.

❋ Designate a place (basket) for students to hand in their finished "little books." Books are not intended to be formally graded/assessed.

❋ Make a "pocket" for finished books by stapling a file folder on the sides and slipping them in after giving them a quick read (to make sure they are finished).

❋ Keep extra books in a basket and give students five more when they finish their first five and so on. Another option is to occasionally have a "book swap" day when students swap any finished little books for new blank ones.

Noah's little book patterned after It's a Tiger. p. 1: Let's swing with the monkeys. Wait! That's not a monkey. I think it's a crocodile. p. 3: Look out! The crocodile might be here.

Transforming Literacy Teaching in the Era of Higher Standards, K–2 © 2015 by Maria P. Walther, Scholastic Teaching Resources

Launching Writing Workshop With Little Books

❋ Read aloud a book about writing. Some of my favorite books for this mini-lesson are *The Library Mouse* (Kirk, 2007) or *Ralph Tells a Story* (Hanlon, 2012).

❋ Demonstrate how you select an idea for your first little book by making a list of possible topics and picking one from the list. Think aloud about past events, books you've read, and so on, so that students can hear your decision-making process.

❋ Begin writing your own little book in front of students. A document camera works well for demonstration writing. Since I know I will have learners' attention for only a few minutes, I will only write the title and maybe the first page, leaving my readers in suspense!

❋ Show children their folder with blank little books, and invite them to begin their first little book. As children are writing, walk around and jot down anecdotal notes to help you decide on future mini-lessons (see the online resources on page 160 for sample anecdotal note sheet). Keep the first writing session short—leave them wanting more time!

❋ The next day, continue to demonstrate writing your own little book. Don't forget to revise and edit as you go. Encourage children to reread their work from the day before and revise before continuing. Select a few children who revised their work to share. This will encourage others to revise the next day. Continue in this fashion until you are ready for a "teacher-guided writing opportunity" such as a personal narrative. (See pages 145–148 for this inquiry experience.)

books, the more I'm convinced of their far-reaching benefits. In the boxes on this page and on page 66, I explain how I make and manage little books and also how I launch the workshop using them.

But before we get to the "how to," I want to explore the "why." Here's what I've noticed as I've observed young writers. Because the books are blank, children have to make a multitude of decisions regarding composition and design. These are the same choices they will later analyze when they think about how an author used illustrations or images to communicate elements of a story or information.

I've had *many* teachers hesitate at the fact that the books are blank with no writing lines. Rest assured, I offer students many opportunities during the day to write on paper with lines. But from the first little book to the last, I want children to be in charge of how much or how little they need to write to communicate their message, where they place the words on the page, how they balance illustrations and words, where they put the title, dedication, back cover blurb, copyright, and more. Children who compose books with all of these essential parts will be much more savvy consumers of books and other printed materials.

I think it is clear to see how the choice of materials can drive the decisions that young writers make. In addition to little books, students are given opportunities to write in journals and on various types of lined paper depending on which genre they are exploring. More details and information about these writing experiences can be found in *Month-by-Month Trait-Based Writing Instruction* (Walther & Phillips, 2009) and in the writing standards-based learning experiences in Chapter 7. Along with carefully-selected materials, it is important that writers are able to choose what they want to write about.

Choice

There has been much written about the importance of choice in writing workshop. As Katie Wood Ray and Lester Laminack remind us, "By definition, writing is about having something to say, and it is the writer's right to decide what this will be, to decide what he or she wants to say" (2001, p. 7). If you view writing as a decision-making process, then it only makes sense that students should be given the freedom to choose their own writing topics. This is not to say that I don't give writers scaffolding and support as they develop their ability to select a topic for writing. One of the most frequently asked questions I hear from teachers is, "What about the kids who want to write about the same topic like Star Wars, Batman, or videogames, over and over again." Here are some quick tips to help children chart new territory:

- When reading aloud, make a point to identify the author and illustrator so that students begin to understand that the books they love were written by real people who get their ideas from a variety of places. Read author's notes, author websites, and share the stories you've heard from authors about their work. From your first read-aloud to your last, carry on a constant running dialogue about the pursuit of ideas.

- When students share an experience or adventure make a point to say, "That would make a great story/book/nonfiction piece," or "You could write about that today, couldn't you?"

- Introduce students to the copyright page of the book. Share that the © symbol means that the book was copyrighted in that year, meaning no one else can write a book exactly like it.

- Show children how they can take a favorite character from their favorite book, movie, or videogame and put that character in a new setting or take a familiar setting and populate it with new characters. Discuss unique structures children could use to write about favorite topics such as instruction manuals for building with Legos or strategies for getting to the highest level in their favorite video game.

- Say things like, "Imagine if Mo Willems only rewrote his favorite movies and videogames, we wouldn't have Elephant and Piggie or the Pigeon! Wouldn't that be terrible?"

Writers Make Decisions—What Should I Write About?

If your students are having difficulty deciding what to write about, this mini-lesson might help. Read aloud a book to spark a discussion about the fact that writers often get ideas from their own lives. Below are some texts to consider.

Memoirs of a Hamster (Scillian, 2013)	In the sequel to *Memoirs of a Goldfish* (2010), Seymour the hamster is content in his cage until Pearl the cat entices him to explore the outside world. He quickly learns that she only wants him outside his cage for one reason—to eat him.
Ralph Tells a Story (Hanlon, 2012)	Ralph can't think of any ideas for his story. After trying everything, including roaming the hallways, he writes his first story. Notice all of Ralph's stories on the back end papers.
Rocket Writes a Story (Hills, 2012)	In the sequel to *How Rocket Learned to Read* (Hills, 2010), Rocket looks for inspiration for a story. Once he finds it, he writes, revises, and shares his story with his new friend Owl.

Invite students to make lists, heart maps, brain maps, or bright ideas charts (see online resources, page 160) of their favorite things and other events in their life that they might want to write about during writing workshop. Store these in their writing workshop folder for future reference.

- When predicting in reading, celebrate predictions that match the clues and make sense but don't match the author's thinking, because those are ideas for children's own writing.

- If we consciously cultivate ideas for writing (see mini-lesson idea on page 68) and offer students ample time to choose topics, their decision making will improve.

Structure

In the previous chapter, I highlighted three tips for providing structure to the reading workshop. They were: be prepared, be flexible, and be present. The same holds true for writing workshop.

- **Be prepared.** Being prepared for writing workshop means gathering mentor texts that will illuminate the language skill, writing trait, or genre. It also means making sure that the students' writing materials are organized in a way that makes sense for them. My students keep their little books in a two-pocket folder that is stored in a plastic bin. When we're working on a specific genre, we keep the materials for that genre in a separate "pocket" made out of a file folder with the edges stapled. I use the exact same materials to write in my demonstrations. As in reading workshop, I also have chart paper, markers, or an interactive whiteboard document ready to record students' thinking, and a plan of which student(s) and/or guided-writing groups I'd like to meet with that day.

- **Be flexible.** Teachable moments only happen if you're flexible. For instance, if students are busy writing, extend the workshop time for a few minutes. If you have many writers who have something brilliant to share, add a bit of extra sharing time. As I said in the last chapter, being flexible and capitalizing on teachable moments means that you don't always accomplish what you've planned for the day or week. That's okay. Remember, let your students' needs and successes serve as your measure for how much you've accomplished.

- **Be present.** When conferring with children, listen carefully to the content of their piece, notice their illustrations, think about the decision-making process that accompanied their work. Then, decide what you can say to the child that will help him or her move forward as a writer. Remember, you are teaching the writer, not just trying to make that particular piece better.

A Few of My Favorite Mentor Texts for Young Writers

It's a Tiger! (LaRochelle, 2012)	Begin reading this boldly illustrated picture book on the front flap and continue to read, notice, and laugh at the young narrator's adventures as he narrowly escapes a tiger again and again!
Oh, No! (Fleming, 2012)	When a frog, mouse, loris, sun bear, and monkey fall into a hole, the tiger is ready to pounce. Then, elephant comes and saves the animals, and tiger falls into the hole. Will the animals help him out? "Oh, no!"
AH HA! (Mack, 2013)	Frog is relaxing in the pond (AAHH!) when he finds a rock (AH HA!). Close behind, there is a boy with a jar poised to catch him (AH HA!), and the chase begins. Using only four letters, Jeff Mack tells a rollicking tale.

Mentor or Expert Support

An experienced writing mentor is at your fingertips every time you open a book. Along with mentor texts, your whole-class demonstrations and conversations with individual writers mentor students as they experiment with new writing techniques. In fact, you are the most influential writer in the room. Each time children watch you struggle to think of an idea, ponder how you want your story to end, or debate how to clearly explain a fact, they are privy to the inner conversation of a writer. More important, they see that writing is challenging—even for adults.

The following Transforming Teaching chart shows how you can enhance your writing workshop.

Enhancing Writing Workshop

TRANSFORMING TEACHING	
Mentor texts are used to highlight writing techniques.	Mentor texts are used to highlight craft and structure from both the writer's and reader's perspective.
Two-way conversations—teacher-student, student-student—are the most prevalent.	Collaborative conversations initiated by students in response to peers' writing, ideas, and suggestions permeate the day.
Separate mini-lessons are based on individual strategies and skills from state standards, district curriculum, or packaged program scope and sequence.	A series of mini-lessons center on big ideas integrated across language arts strands (reading, writing, speaking, listening, viewing/visually representing).
Spelling is only taught as a separate subject or during a separate block.	Spelling strategies are integrated into writing workshop.
Writing strategies or writing traits are the organizing features.	Overarching themes, big ideas, and genres are the organizing features, with writing strategies or traits used as tools to strengthen writing.
The study of grammar and conventions are often taught outside the writing workshop.	The study of grammar and conventions are integrated into the writing workshop.
The writing genres studied often include narrative, persuasive, and expository.	The writing genres studied include narrative, opinion, and informational/explanatory text, and under these broad genres, writers learn about many different ways to communicate in each genre.
Guiding writers mainly occurs in a whole-class setting or one-on-one.	Guiding writers occurs individually or in small, needs-based groups.
Students write independently while the teacher engages in other activities.	"Independent" writing is structured by conditions, such as explicit instruction and teacher monitoring, to increase students' accountability and strengthen their writing.
Sharing is focused on *what* writers did or learned.	Sharing and celebration are focused on reflections about *how* writers went about crafting their pieces—the process or strategies that were independently applied.

Workshop Components

Establishing mirroring reading and writing workshop components will transform your literacy instruction in these ways:

- Demonstrate the connection between reading and writing.

- Teach students to read like writers and write like readers as you study texts from both the reader's and writer's point of view.

- Create seamless transitions because students know exactly what to expect as they shift from one workshop to the other.

- Provide opportunities to plan series of integrated mini-lessons centering on big ideas or topics.

- Allow more time to teach foundational and language skills in meaningful contexts.

As you continue reading this chapter, I'll show you how each component of the workshop addresses a particular goal found in the standards, and more important, how the components work in concert to support young writers by providing a balanced approach to writing instruction.

Read Aloud Like a Writer

> **Mentor or Expert Support** → *Mentor texts are used to highlight craft and structure from both the writer's and reader's perspective.*

If you're a children's book fanatic like I am, I'll bet you can quickly rattle off some books you love to read aloud—books that compel your students to shout, "Read it again!" There's a reason that certain read-alouds become favorites. The author and illustrator have worked their magic to create a unique reading experience. It's the magic that we want to highlight and make visible to our students—the craft techniques that authors and illustrators use to make their work distinctive. That is what "reading like a writer" is all about. For young writers, we also want to consider noticing and naming techniques that they can easily incorporate into their own writing or illustrations. So, we look for books that include craft techniques such as:

- Various text structures
- Sensory language
- Creative conventions
- Repetition
- Word play
- Onomatopoeia

Establish mirroring workshop components to help learners connect reading and writing.

A Quick Look at the Components of a K–2 Writing Workshop

- ❋ Read Aloud Like a Writer
- ❋ Collaborative Conversations
- ❋ Mini-Lessons
  - Words for Writers
  - Writing Strategy Instruction
  - Grammar Study
  - Genre Awareness
- ❋ Guiding Writers Individually or in Small Groups
- ❋ "Independent" Writing
- ❋ Sharing and Celebrating

- Interjections
- Speech bubbles
- Illustration techniques

In the Common Core Reading Standards, there is a strand labeled craft and structure. To me, this is the "read like a writer" strand. When we show children how to read from the perspective of an author, we are not only helping to strengthen their writing skills, but also helping them to comprehend texts better.

Mentor Texts for Young Writers

When selecting a mentor text, look for the following craft techniques:

Craft Technique	Mentor Text Suggestions
VARIOUS TEXT STRUCTURES	(See page 146 for a list of texts with various structures.)
SENSORY LANGUAGE	*Winter Is Coming* (Johnston, 2014)—While watching animals from a platform in a tree, a young girl describes what she observes on her visits to the edge of the woods from September through late November.
CREATIVE CONVENTIONS	*Rooting for You: A Moving Up Story* (Hood, 2014)—Bud the seed is reluctant to sprout and grow until his underground friends support him and cheer him on.
REPETITION	*Snowflakes Fall* (MacLachlan, 2013)—MacLachlan's poetic text and repetition of the words "snowflakes fall" make this book an ideal mentor text.
WORD PLAY	*Froodle* (Portis, 2014)—Find out what happens when an inventive little brown bird decides that rather than peeping he will sing his own silly song.
ONOMATOPOEIA	*Storm Song* (Viau, 2013)—Experience the sounds of a summer thunderstorm from beginning to end.
SPEECH BUBBLES	*Frog and Fly: Six Slurpy Stories* (Mack, 2012)—With one or two simple cartoons per page, Mack tells the story of a hungry frog and a delicious fly. This book is ideal for pointing out the difference between speech bubbles and thought bubbles.
ILLUSTRATION TECHNIQUES	*This Is a Moose* (Morris, 2014)—Director Duck is trying to make a film about a moose doing "moose things" but discovers that moose has other plans. Tom Lichtenheld's illustrations are filled with interesting details to notice and discuss.

Collaborative Conversations

> **Collaborative Conversations** → *Collaborative conversations initiated by students in response to peers' writing, ideas, and suggestions permeate the day.*

Every day, young writers make decisions. They make decisions about the texts they choose to write, the approaches they take to writing that text, what to do when they come to a word they don't know how to spell, and so on. To move students closer to the overarching goal of writing effectively in various genres and for various audiences, we engage in "read like a writer" conversations. These text-focused discussions occur as students are immersed in narrative, informational, and opinion pieces written by both published and student authors. By listening to and discussing mentor texts, students will learn how writers make decisions and how these decisions impact the reader. They will also develop a better understanding of genre, purpose, and audience. In the box at right, you'll find some questions and comments to start your conversations. Collaborative conversations surrounding mentor texts often lead right into your mini-lesson because the purpose of a writing mini-lesson is to teach learners something that they can use to make their writing stronger.

Mini-Lessons

> **Mini-Lessons** → *A series of mini-lessons is centered on big ideas integrated across language arts strands (reading, writing, speaking, listening, viewing/visually representing).*

Mini-lessons are, and always will be, a vital component of the workshop. It is a consistent, daily time to explicitly showcase specific aspects of literacy instruction. During the writing workshop, mini-lessons usually focused on the following aspects:

- Words for Writers
- Writing Strategy Instruction
- Grammar Study
- Genre Awareness

A way to transform instruction during mini-lessons is to take a wide-angle view of the lessons. Instead of planning each mini-lesson as a separate entity, consider the end goal or big idea that you want your students to be able to do and know. Using the standards, which are written as end-of-year goals, we design a series of mini-lessons to teach the prerequisite skills, strategies, and habits of mind to reach that particular end destination.

The Language of "Read Like a Writer" Conversations

❋ Did you hear the way the author chose to write that line? Let's listen to it again! Why do you think [the author] chose to write it that way?

❋ How did those words make you feel as a reader?

❋ Let me read that part again. Listen to the [rhythm, repeated line, alliteration, rhyme]. Why do you think [the author] chose to use that technique here? Could you do something like that in your own writing?

❋ Who is telling the story right here? How did [the author] communicate that to you as a reader?

❋ What is [the author] trying to teach you here? Is [the author] using words or illustrations/ text features? Did that help you understand? How might you go about doing the same thing in your own piece?

Sample Mini-Lesson Series

1. Introduce the concept. Share and discuss concrete examples using a mentor text or mentor sentences.

2. Notice and discuss how authors use this feature in their own writing.

3. Apply the concept to different contexts.

4. Invite students to try it in their own writing.

5. Share and celebrate writers' experimentation and approximations.

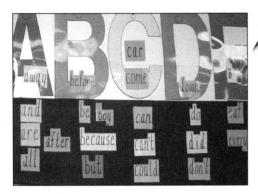

Teach, practice, and regularly review high-frequency words using the word wall.

Strategies for Supporting Beginning Spellers

❋ Encourage the use of developmental spelling and refrain from spelling words for children.

❋ Demonstrate and practice how to sound out and spell words using known sounds and spelling patterns.

❋ Teach, practice, and regularly review high-frequency words using the word wall approach developed by Patricia Cunningham (2009).

❋ Expect that known high-frequency words posted on the word wall and words with known spelling patterns are spelled conventionally.

❋ Create a plan for whole-class, systematic word-study instruction.

❋ Incorporate differentiated word-study instruction into guided reading.

WORDS FOR WRITERS

Words For Writers → *Spelling strategies are integrated into writing workshop.*

Words for writers is a "means by which we help our students to apply their growing knowledge of phonics to their written work" (Walther & Phillips, 2009, p. 11). Simply stated, we do not spell words for our young writers. Instead, we use a multifaceted approach for teaching students how to spell words on their own. A list of the teaching strategies we use to support students as they move toward meeting Language Anchor Standard 2 appears in the box at left.

Certainly, the ability to sound out and spell words is an essential aspect of writing instruction for young learners. But convention-focused writing instruction will not help students develop an understanding of how to put those words together to clearly communicate a message. That's where the language of the traits helps support writers as they craft and revise their pieces.

WRITING STRATEGY INSTRUCTION

Writing Strategy Instruction → *Overarching themes, big ideas, and genres are the organizing features, with writing strategies or traits used as tools to strengthen writing.*

Wise teachers like you determine the content of their mini-lessons based on students' needs and the expectations set forth in the standards. As you unpack the standards, you'll discover that the language of the traits will be helpful when discussing quality writing and will give you a sensible structure for organizing your mini-lessons. For example, the introduction to the Common Core writing standards states, "Each year in writing, students should demonstrate increasing sophistication in all aspects of language use from vocabulary (word choice) and syntax (fluency) to the development (ideas) and organization (organization) of ideas" (p. 19). This occurs in a writing workshop environment where students care about what they are writing and, in turn, want to strengthen their writing by revising. In the box on page 75, I've unpacked specific examples where the language of the writing traits is woven into the standards document. Then, in the teaching routine on pages 75–76 and the boxes on page 75–78, I offer exemplar texts for integrating conventions during interactive writing and tips for teaching conventions during editing conversations.

 Transforming Literacy Teaching in the Era of Higher Standards, K–2 © 2015 by Maria P. Walther, Scholastic Teaching Resources

Integrating Conventions During Interactive Writing

TARGETS

- I can show you how words work.
- I can show you how sentences work.

PREPARATION

When preparing text for interactive writing, write large enough so that it's visible to all of your students and position the text low enough to write so that they can interact with it to apply their new learning. The following materials work well for interactive writing:

- Chart Paper
- Chalkboard or Whiteboard
- Markers
- Interactive Whiteboard

EXPLANATION

Interactive writing helps teach children about the way we write down spoken language. While composing a piece of writing, select individual students to assist you in writing letters, words, or phrases depending on their ability. Thus, you and your students write together using a shared pen to create conventional pieces of text for students to read and refer to at a later date. Some possible interactive writing experiences include these:

- Revising and editing the morning message
- Writing about class experiences and activities
- Recording facts learned during science and social studies investigations
- Creating a story summary
- Writing a book review
- Composing anchor charts
- Rewriting familiar texts
- Labeling graphs and charts (Walther & Phillips, 2009)

EXPERIENCE

Day 1

- Establish a purpose and audience for writing.
- Brainstorm ideas for creating the text.
- Co-write the text using a shared pen.
- Model and discuss spacing, return sweep, capitalization, and punctuation.

The Trait Language of Ideas and the Common Core State Standards

- ❋ Use a combination of drawing, dictating, and writing to compose or narrate. (W.K.1/2/3)
- ❋ Recall information from experiences or gather information from provided sources to answer a question. (W.K/1/2.8)
- ❋ Focus on a topic. (W.1/2.5)
- ❋ Include some details regarding what happened. (W.1.3)
- ❋ Include details to describe actions, thoughts, and feelings. (W.2.3)
- ❋ Add details to strengthen writing as needed. (W.K/1.5)

Day 2

- Reread, revise, and edit the text.

Day 3

- Revisit the text and focus on key vocabulary words and phonetic features of individual words.
- Summarize and reflect on the learning that occurred.

Day 4

- Extend the experience by placing the text in the classroom library for further enjoyment (Walther & Phillips, 2009). To extend this learning experience, provide plenty of time for learners to write. Invite children to read aloud their own written work, asking them to point to each word as they read.

The traits are powerful because they provide concrete, common language to use when discussing writing. When you teach focused mini-lessons using trait language and continue to use the trait language when you read like a writer and confer with writers, you'll notice children begin to use the terms *ideas, word choice, organization, fluency, voice,* and *conventions* as they discuss written words.

A Few Exemplar Texts to Highlight Conventions

Goal! (Taylor, 2014)
Stunning photographs of children from across the globe playing soccer.
Convention: Commas in a series

The Woods (Hoppe, 2011)
A boy heads to the woods to search for his stuffed bear.
Convention: Ellipses

If You Were a Dog (Swenson, 2014)
Young listeners think about what kind of animal they would like to be as they hear the bouncy, rhythmic text.
Convention: Dashes

GRAMMAR STUDY

Grammar Study → *The study of grammar and conventions is integrated into the writing workshop.*

The language standards include the essential "rules" of standard written and spoken English, but they also approach language as a matter of craft and informed choice among alternatives. In their review of research on teaching grammar, Michael Smith and Jeff Wilhelm (2006) share some valuable information to guide your thinking in terms of grammar instruction:

- Grammar lessons should occur in the context of written or spoken language.
- Grammar instruction should make sense to students.
- Grammar instruction should be viewed as a way to improve students' writing.

For practical advice in putting this research into classroom practice, I turn to Jeff Anderson's book *Mechanically Inclined* (2005). He reminds us that instead of teaching grammar and mechanics by using what he calls daily "correct-alls," where students are given a sentence riddled with errors and asked to edit the sentence, we teach grammar the same way we teach other craft techniques, as follows:

- Teach the grammar kids need to know. (You can't teach everything at once!)
- Immerse students in correct models visually and orally. (Select mentor sentences from texts to demonstrate how authors use possessive nouns, conjunctions, prepositions, and so on.)
- Demonstrate how you apply grammar in your own writing.
- Post anchor charts that provide reinforcement of the concepts you've introduced and practiced.

Teaching Conventions With Editing Conversations

We know that conventions are important, but sometimes we spend so much time focused on them that we lose sight of the real goal of writing—to communicate thoughts and feelings. Craft-focused instruction means that when you confer with a student or assess his or her writing, you begin by noticing the craft decisions or the deliberate choices the writer has made. Focus on *reading* the words and pictures for content first. How does the piece sound? Does it make sense? Then, when you're talking about editing for conventions, you can use the tips below to guide your editing conversation and help young writers develop an awareness of conventions, the willingness to experiment, and the patience to take a second look at their written work

TIP #1: START SMALL

Start with age-appropriate, everyday editing tasks. For example, encourage students to check that they've written their name on the paper. To introduce editing say, "Boys and girls, each time you write something you will put your name on your paper. Before we put our papers away, I will remind you to go back and edit your paper. That means you should check for your name." Notice and celebrate that students had the patience to go back and look for this detail! Add other simple editing tasks like:

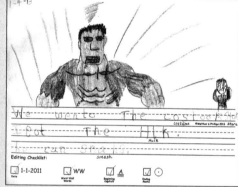

- Edit to see if the first word you wrote begins with a capital.

- Edit to see if the last word you wrote has an ending mark.

- Edit to see if the word *I* is capitalized.

- Edit to see if your friends' names begin with a capital.

- Edit to see if every ending mark is followed by a beginning capital.

Start with age-appropriate editing tasks.

TIP #2: THINK AND TALK LIKE EDITORS

To help reinforce the thinking behind the conventions, demonstrate the use of conventions in the morning message and during shared writing. Explain why you use each convention. Then, as students begin to create their own conventional text (multiple words, beginning sentences, punctuated phrases and sentences), get in the habit of regularly asking for the reason behind using a particular convention.

- Why did you put a [period, question mark, exclamation mark] here? How do you want your reader to say this sentence?

- What do you want your readers to do here? If you want them to pause, insert a comma.

- What signal are you giving to your reader?

TIP #3: CELEBRATE DISCOVERIES

When a child discovers the period and puts one at the end of every line (or every word!), instead of worrying about correctness (at this stage) celebrate by saying, "Wow! Roshan, I see you've discovered periods! You have a lot of them in your writing now!"

TIP #4: POINT OUT WHAT STUDENTS ARE DOING RIGHT

Make sure your students know what they are doing well. Congratulate them for using left-right orientation, remembering spaces between words, sounding out words carefully, or producing readable spelling. Celebrate the little victories.

TIP #5: USE ENVIRONMENTAL PRINT, BOOKS, AND DIGITAL MEDIA TO HIGHLIGHT CONVENTIONS

- Why do you think the writer used a capital here?
- What does this mark (point to punctuation mark) mean?
- This print is in all capital letters. Why do you think the writer did that?
- This writer put a picture here. Was that a good idea?
- Writers often use titles. Why? Do they help?

(Adapted from: Seeing With New Eyes: A Guidebook on Teaching and Assessing Beginning Writers [Northwest Regional Educational Laboratory, 1999])

Post anchor charts to reinforce grammar concepts.

GENRE AWARENESS

> **Genre Awareness →** *The writing genres studied include narrative, opinion, and informational/ explanatory text, and under these broad genres writers learn about many different ways to communicate in each genre.*

Of course, we want students to gain experience with the three broad genres—opinion, narrative, and explanatory/informational—that the standards have identified, but there are many kinds of writing that fall under those categories. As the writing world is rapidly expanding, one thing is for sure, our students will be writing in genre formats that don't even exist today. To think, less than a decade ago, few people had heard of text messages, blog posts, and tweets. We also know that most effective writing is mixed-genre writing. For instance, when writing your opinion, you might include a narrative section to connect with the reader, or an informational piece might include the writer's opinion about the topic. To increase students' genre awareness, teach mini-lessons that achieve the following:

- Encourage wide reading
- Expose writers to the various digital media and genres found in the classroom, school, or public library

Transforming Literacy Teaching in the Era of Higher Standards, K–2 © 2015 by Maria P. Walther, Scholastic Teaching Resources

- Attend to author's purpose
- Analyze text structures
- Notice how authors approach a genre
- Compare and contrast different genres
- Apply craft techniques to their own writing

Providing young writers with an extensive knowledge of the various genres and text structures that they might use when communicating their ideas not only helps them make informed decisions as writers, but also helps them read with a more critical stance.

Guiding Writers

Guiding Writers → *Guiding writers occurs individually or in small, needs-based groups.*

Because the reading and writing workshops have parallel processes, you can use many of the same tactics that you use to guide readers when you are coaching writers. For instance, after the mini-lesson, instead of sending students out to read books, send them out to write books. During this "independent" writing time, support writers with individual or small-group conferences. (For more information on small-group conferring see *Month-by-Month Trait-Based Writing Instruction* [Walther & Phillips, 2009].) As with all the routines you establish in your classroom, you'll want to co-create an anchor chart with your students like the one on this page, detailing your expectations for this time.

"Independent" Writing

"Independent" Writing → *"Independent" writing is structured by conditions, such as explicit instruction and teacher monitoring, to increase students' accountability and strengthen their writing.*

You'll notice the word "independent" is in quotation marks. The reason for that is twofold. First, when you teach young learners, it takes a lot of modeling and support to help them independently engage in any activity. Second, because independent writing is only as successful as the conditions that surround it. (See box on page 80.)

As you can see, the conditions that support independent writing parallel those that surround the workshop.

Each day during independent writing, take a moment to look up from your conference or guided-writing group.

What does guided writing look like?

❋ Students choose their own perfect writing space. (Note: *Some writers may need guidance to select a place to work.*)

❋ Children write individually, in pairs, triads, or small groups.

❋ Teacher circulates or confers with individuals or small groups.

What does guided writing sound like?

❋ Children stretch out/sound out words for writing.

❋ Students reread texts orally to figure out what to write next, to listen for fluency, to revise, and to edit.

❋ Writers read to their friends or engage in writing-related discussions.

(Adapted from Month-by-Month Trait-Based Writing Instruction *[Walther & Phillips, 2009])*

As you look around, notice those children who are engaged and those who aren't. Jot down the names of the unengaged children so that you can bring them together to brainstorm possible writing topics or offer strategies for building their stamina. This check-in is essential to ensuring that students are using their independent writing time wisely. As with all aspects of writing workshop, independent writing flourishes with an intentional focus on classroom culture and the continued monitoring of students' progress by conferring with writers on a regular basis.

Guide writers to engage in writing-related discussions.

Critical Classroom Conditions for Effective Independent Writing

❋ **Time**—Daily in-class time to write

❋ **Choice**—Student-selected topics

❋ **Explicit instruction**—Mini-lessons and demonstrations on what, why, and how writers write

❋ **Volume and variety**—Students gain experience writing a wide variety of genres

❋ **Teacher monitoring**—Brief, teacher-initiated individual student conferences

❋ **Collaborative conversations**— Partner and small-group discussions to give feedback to strengthen writing

(Adapted from Miller & Moss [2013, p. 16])

CONFERRING

When children are writing in little books and you are using the anecdotal notes sheet (found in the online resources; see page 160), consider the following questions as you jot down your observations while conferring with writers. These observations will serve as an informal, formative assessment of student writing.

Ideas

- What decisions do you observe the writer making? Is the writer able to communicate his or her reasons behind the craft decisions?

- Is the writer revising? Is the student able to take suggestions and make revisions in his or her writing?

- Is he or she applying craft techniques noticed in mentor texts and content from mini-lessons in his or her writing?

- Does the student write about a variety of topics/ideas?

- Is the student able to generate an idea independently?

- Does the student include details in his or her illustrations/writing?

Organization

- How has the writer organized his or her book? Has the writer used one of the predictable patterns that you've shared or something he or she learned from another mentor text?

- **Fiction:** Does the little book have a clear beginning, middle, and end? Does the student's text/illustration include interesting details?

- **Informational:** Does the little book stick to one topic? Does the text/illustration include interesting details?

Conventions

- Does the writer edit for ending punctuation?

- Does the writer edit for beginning capitalization?

- What is the student's stage of spelling development?

- Does the writer spell word-wall words correctly?

Transforming Literacy Teaching in the Era of Higher Standards, K–2 © 2015 by Maria P. Walther, Scholastic Teaching Resources

Sharing and Celebrating

> **Sharing and Celebrating** → *Sharing and celebration are focused on reflections about how writers went about crafting their pieces—the process or strategies that were independently applied.*

Think about the last time you were asked to share something you've written in front of your peers. I'm guessing that experience might have made your heart race a bit. Were you reluctant? Did you avoid the situation by going to the bathroom?! Before you ask students to share what they have written, you want to ensure that you've created a safe, non-threatening environment where this will take place. You want sharing time to be a time to celebrate your writers' accomplishments. To do this, engage in a conversation with students about sharing written work. Ask and record responses to the questions below that you feel might help your students articulate the norms they want to set for sharing.

- Who do you like to share your writing with?
- How does it make you feel to share your writing?
- How does it make you feel when others comment on your writing?
- What kinds of comments are helpful in improving your writing? (See box at right for some helpful comments and questions for writers.)
- What kinds of questions are helpful in improving your writing?
- Why is it important to be an active listener?
- How can you be an active listener?

Helpful Comments and Questions for Writers

In her book *Creating Young Writers* (Spandel, 2007, pp. 123–124), Vicki Spandel suggests teaching students the following kinds of comments and questions that are helpful to a writer.

※ Tell the writer something you noticed.

※ Name a favorite word or phrase. Say, "My favorite word (or phrase) was . . ."

※ Describe something you pictured in your mind as you were listening.

※ Name something [a person, place, experience, or another book] you were reminded of while listening to the piece.

※ Are you curious about what will happen next? Say, "I'm curious about what will happen after . . . "

※ Did anything surprise you? What? Say, "I was surprised when . . ."

※ Did the voice in the text sound like the writer's speaking voice? If so, let the writer know.

Once you've collaborated to create class norms, demonstrate and practice them. With guidance and support, students will learn how to listen to their peers' feedback and use it to help make their writing better. Establishing a collaborative community of writers right from the start sets the foundation for the rest of the year.

Looking Back, Moving Forward

Writing with young learners is challenging and rewarding. After many years of doing it, I can say that the workshop model has saved me on many a day. The predictable structures, clear expectations, and intentional teaching fosters independence and creates a collaborative writing community. In this community, young writers know how important it is to learn from and support each other. I'm just one of the many writers in the room trying every day to learn something new that is going to make my writing even better!

As you transition from Part 1 to Part 2, you will continue to transform your teaching by adding teaching routines (Chapter 5) and inquiry experiences (Chapters 6 and 7) to the new essentials for literacy teaching that you learned about in Part 1. Each teaching routine and inquiry experience addresses the essence or big idea of a key teaching goal, along with specific learning targets. As you guide students through these routines and experiences, revisit the overarching, cross-curricular targets I identified in Chapter 2 (see box on page 83). These are the ultimate goals for students who are independent, self-directed learners.

When you weave these routines and experiences into your reading and writing workshops, you will not only be reaching higher standards but also encouraging your students to be thoughtful readers and writers who embody the literacy practices outlined in Chapter 2:

- Make sense of words and persevere in figuring them out.

- Reason abstractly and qualitatively.

- Construct logical, evidence-based arguments and critique the reasoning of others.

- Think by writing.

- Use structure of text, text features, and digital resources strategically.

- Comprehend and communicate with precision.

- Look for and make use of structure.

To help with your planning, the description of both teaching routines and inquiry experiences follows the same format. (See box at left.) For many of the routines and experiences, you will find a suggested text or two that will lead learners to the essential understandings. Keep in mind these texts are not the only resources you can use. I'm sure you have a shelf of books or a collection of online resources that work well for teaching certain lessons or concepts. As you read through the experiences in this part of the book, think about where those tried-and-true texts will enhance the experience. More important, when selecting books, consider your students' interests and learning needs.

The Components of Teaching Routines and Inquiry Experiences

Each teaching routine and inquiry experience description contains these elements:

❋ **Target(s):** Learning targets, written in kid-friendly language, will lead students toward key understandings that are rooted in the essential questions based on my unpacking of the standards; see pp. 23–24. Targets set the stage for the experience and help students understand the significance of the learning.

❋ **Preparation:** Here I will tell you everything you need to facilitate your inquiry experience. Often, you will find carefully-selected book titles that can serve as exemplar texts as you add books from your own collection.

❋ **Explanation:** The explanation found in this section is for you. It is the "why" behind the experience. This rationale might come in handy for conversations with your students' families, administrators, or when you are documenting your decision-making process as you engage in the teacher evaluation process.

❋ **Experience:** Most of the learning experiences contained in this chapter are ongoing explorations. Like separate threads that, when woven together, create a rich tapestry of instruction, the big ideas that children will gain from engaging in these experiences over time will blend together to create learners who exemplify the portrait of students we reviewed in Chapter 1.

Chapter 5

Teaching Routines

Transforming Teaching Routines

The teaching routines that follow are designed to be joyful, purposeful, and ongoing. They will span your entire year and help you do the following:

- Enhance read-aloud experiences
- Make thinking visible
- Integrate foundational and language skills
- Spotlight vivid vocabulary

With a clear end goal in mind (see the learning targets), you will be teaching skills and strategies within authentic reading and writing experiences. As you read this section of the book and transform these

Go online to view a video on Teaching Routines in Action; see page 160.

Overarching Cross-Curricular Learning Targets

* I can PAUSE.
* I can PONDER.
* I can look for PATTERNS.
* I can PROBLEM SOLVE.
* I can be PRECISE.
* I can communicate my PROCESS.
* I can PERSEVERE.

teaching practices, it is up to you to teach responsively, continually adjusting the routines based on the results of your formative assessments and the needs and interests of your students. When you fine-tune each instructional practice with your learners in mind, the experiences will become even more relevant, interesting, and challenging.

Big Idea: Enhance Read-Aloud Experiences

First and foremost, read-alouds should be pleasurable, community-building experiences. We read aloud because we want students to *love* books and to internalize the rhythms and cadences of written language. But knowing that every minute counts, it is wise to naturally weave in conversations that address specific learning targets. The next five teaching routines will show you how to enhance your read-aloud experiences in ways that keep them joyful and engaging. With practice, these routines will become part of your teaching repertoire, and you will begin to incorporate these learning targets, and many more, on your own.

Highlight the Roles of Author and Illustrator

TARGETS

- I can explain what an author does.
- I can explain what an illustrator does.
- I can use what I've learned in my own writing.

PREPARATION

Become familiar with your favorite authors and illustrators. To do this, you can simply check out their websites or follow them on Twitter. Find out how to pronounce their names. If you have opportunities to meet published authors, take a picture with them and glue it inside their books so that you can show it to your students.

EXPLANATION

When students understand that the author and illustrator are real people, they are better at figuring out the author's purpose and point of view. The role of the author and illustrator has more meaning to children who see themselves as writers and illustrators. This underscores the importance of offering students the opportunities to make little books, as discussed in Chapter 4.

EXPERIENCE

Each time you read a book aloud, be prepared to read the author's and illustrator's names. If there's time, share a little bit about them. It can be something simple like, "Did you know that Tom Lichtenheld lives in Geneva, Illinois? That's not far from our school!" or "The illustrator Chris Soentpiet creates all of his illustrations using live models. Can you tell by looking at them?" Your aim here is to make these people come alive for your students.

While reading aloud, discuss the role of the author and illustrator. Pose questions to spark conversations:

- Where do you think [the author] got his or her ideas for this book?

- Why do you think [the author] wrote this book? To make us laugh, help us learn, or make us ponder?

- How do you think the author gathered the facts for this informational text?

- How do you think this illustrator created these illustrations? (Note: This information is often found on the copyright page.)

- If you saw another book illustrated by [the illustrator], would you recognize his or her style?

- Did the illustrations help you better understand the words?

Identify the Parts of a Book

TARGETS

- I can notice and name the different parts of a book.

- I can think about how the illustrator's and/or book designer's decisions impact my experience as a reader.

- I can use the same techniques in my own writing.

PREPARATION

Take a moment to look at the hardcover books you were already planning to read aloud and notice if they have most or all of the parts listed in the chart on page 86. If so, use one of those books. If not, find some that do.

EXPLANATION

Why is it important that students know how to identify book parts and use the terms as they converse about books and write their own? Because eventually, we want learners to be able to analyze the structure of the text, explain how the parts relate to one another and to the whole, and think about structure as they organize their own pieces. We might begin this conversation in the primary grades by noticing how a close look at the cover can build a bit of background before we read the book or how reading the back-flap bio can tell us a little about the author. As we highlight each part, we explain how it helps us as readers. Soon, students take over this responsibility in noticing and naming the parts of a book and sharing their thoughts on how they support the reader.

Point out and discuss the different parts of a book.

EXPERIENCE

While reading aloud, point out and discuss the different parts of a book.
Build students' understanding of composition and the decision-making process by asking the following questions:

- Why do you think [the author/illustrator] chose to do it this way?

- How did noticing that part help you as a reader?

- How might you do something like that in your own book? Why?

A Few of My Favorite Books With Distinctive Examples

Cover	Exemplar Book
WRAP-AROUND COVER	*Fossil* (Thomson, 2013)—Readers have to "unwrap" or view both the front and back cover at the same time to see the whole illustration.
COVER AND SPINE	*Exclamation Mark* (Rosenthal, 2013)—See if your students notice what is unique about the cover of this book. Hint: It does not contain a title in words—just the image of the exclamation mark! Then, turn to the spine to show learners the title.
TITLE PAGE	*A Mouse That Says Moo* (Hamburg, 2013)—Begin reading this book by looking carefully at the title page and noticing the items strewn around the yard. Each appears in this rhyming tale of a girl's imaginary zoo.
DEDICATION PAGE	*Saturdays and Teacakes* (Laminack, 2004)—"In memory of Zella Mozelle Thompson, my Mammaw (who would know that every word of this is true) . . ." Notice that this memoir is dedicated to the person it is about.
FRONT FLAP	*It's a Tiger* (LaRochelle, 2012)—If you start reading this book on the front flap it makes it even more fun.
BACK FLAP	*Super Hair-o and the Barber of Doom* (Rocco, 2013)— John Rocco's photo and bio are hilarious!
BACK-COVER BLURB	*Badger's Fancy Meal* (Kasza, 2007)—This back-cover blurb, "You never know what you've got till it's gone," reveals the big idea of the book and leads to an interesting after-reading discussion.
GUTTER	*This Book Just Ate My Dog!* (Byrne, 2014)—When Bella takes her dog for a "stroll across the page," he disappears into the gutter of the book along with her friend, the rescue squad, and Bella herself. Quick thinking Bella writes a note to the readers telling them to shake the book and get everyone out.

Introduce a Variety of Genres

TARGET

I can read and write many different types of texts.

PREPARATION

- Create a reading interest survey or use a published one like the one found in *Next Step Guided Reading Assessment* (Richardson & Walther, 2013).

- Prepare an ongoing genre anchor chart or interactive whiteboard document like the one found on page 87 to chart and discuss the various genres that you read aloud and that students might try their hand at writing.

- Assemble a text set that includes a variety of genres. For multi-genre texts sets, see page 47.

GENRES WE READ AND WRITE

* <u>Biographies</u>: Biographers teach us true facts and interesting details about a part or all of a person's life.

* <u>Modern Fantasy</u>: When authors create an imaginary world—sometimes filled with magic and a talking animal or two—it is called fantasy.

* <u>Graphic Novels</u>: Combining words and pictures in the style of a comic book, writers of graphic novels create a series of illustrations which, when read in order, tell a story.

* <u>Historical Fiction</u>: Authors of historical fiction write stories about people, places, and events set in a world that exists in the past.

* <u>Informational Texts</u>: Informational text writers do research to find true and up-to-date facts to teach us about our world.

* <u>Poetry</u>: Long or short, happy or sad, the words poets choose help us see things in a different way.

* <u>Realistic Fiction</u>: When authors write a story that never happened, but could happen in real life, they are writing realistic fiction.

* <u>Science Fiction</u>: Futuristic fiction writers tell a story set in the future and based on scientific facts.

* <u>Traditional Tales</u>: Long ago people told these tales and they were passed down from one generation to the next. Finally, authors began to write them down, and now we get to enjoy many different versions of folk tales, fairy tales, and fables from all over the world.

EXPLANATION

We present different genres and text types during our read-alouds for a variety of purposes, including the following:

* Introduce real-world texts and digital media
* Ponder the author's purpose
* Analyze different text structures in order to better understand the content
* Explore interconnectedness among texts on similar topics
* Provide ideas for writing
* Discover books that match interests
* Share opinions

EXPERIENCE

Children's ability to read and write a variety of texts depends on how much exposure they have had to books and other

Ask students to rate books on a scale of one to four stars.

reading materials. To help them expand their literary horizons, we need to dedicate ourselves to introducing them to the wide world of books, and one of the best ways to do this is through read-alouds.

- Assess your classroom library. Ask yourself, "Do my books reflect my students' interests?"
- Introduce students to a wide range of authors, books in a series, genres, and digital resources. As you introduce each genre, add it to the genre anchor chart. This chart will serve as a helpful reminder to students as they discover the diverse reading materials that are available to them and the types of texts they might choose to write.
- Ask students to rate books on a scale of one to four stars, similar to a movie review. Invite students to share their rating and rationale. At first, young readers tend to give every book four stars, but as the year progresses and you share your own ratings, they get more discriminating and are better able to support their opinion with evidence from the text.

Compare and Contrast Fiction and Nonfiction

TARGETS

- I can notice and name the parts of a fiction text.
- I can use what I've learned when reading and writing fiction texts.
- I can notice and name the parts of an informational text.
- I can use what I've learned when reading and writing informational texts.
- I can compare and contrast fiction and nonfiction books.

PREPARATION

When selecting read-alouds, texts for guided reading, or books to put in students' book boxes, search for fiction and informational pairings that highlight the differences in craft and structure between the two texts. See the chart of exemplar texts below.

FICTION	INFORMATIONAL
Aaaarrgghh! Spider (Monks, 2004)	*Spiders* (Bishop, 2007)
Bear Snores On (Wilson, 2002)	*Hibernation* (Kosara, 2011)
Butterfly Tree (Markle, 2011)	*A Butterfly Is Patient* (Aston, 2011)
Chicken Big (Graves, 2010)	*Where Do Chicks Come From?* (Sklansky, 2005)
I'm a Frog! (Willems, 2013)	*Frogs!* (Carney, 2009)
Superworm (Donaldson, 2012)	*Wiggling Worms at Work* (Pfeffer, 2004)
Tiger in My Soup (Sheth, 2013)	*Tigers* (Marsh, 2012)
What the Ladybug Heard (Donaldson, 2010)	*Ladybugs* (Gibbons, 2012)

EXPLANATION

The increased emphasis on informational text in the primary-grade classroom is not a new focus that began with the Common Core State Standards. Over a decade ago, in her study of first-grade classrooms, researcher Nell Duke found that children spent an average of 3.6 minutes a day with informational text (2000). She, and many other experts in the field who followed her lead, called for more informational text in primary-grade classrooms. One way to integrate nonfiction throughout the year is by reading aloud and comparing paired fiction and nonfiction texts. This teaching routine helps students discern the difference between fiction and informational texts, understand the author's purpose for each type of writing, and become familiar with various text structures. As you are incorporating informational texts, note the benefits it has for your students (Norton, 2003):

- Boosts engagement and enjoyment
- Addresses children's interests and questions
- Expands learners' academic vocabularies
- Builds knowledge about topics of interest
- Models how to think and write like a scientist by using the scientific method
- Encourages children to wonder and investigate
- Develops critical reading and thinking skills
- Instills habits of mind like curiosity and careful observation that sustain science
- Informs readers about values, beliefs, lifestyles, and behaviors that are different from their own

---

Questions to Spark Conversations When Comparing Fiction and Nonfiction Texts

- ❋ Who are the authors and illustrators of each text? What is their job?
- ❋ How are these two texts alike? How are they different?
- ❋ What was the author's purpose for writing each text?
- ❋ Why do you think he or she chose this particular approach to the topic?
- ❋ Which text did you prefer? Why? Does anyone have a different opinion?
- ❋ How can you use what you've learned from reading and thinking about these texts in your own writing?

EXPERIENCE

Begin an ongoing, yearlong conversation about the difference between books that tell stories and books that give information using the questions in the box above. Read a pair of books and compare and contrast the texts from both a reader's and a writer's point of view. Invite students to identify and explain the difference between the two text types. Record their thinking on an anchor chart or interactive whiteboard document to refer to and expand on as you continue to read paired texts. In addition, you may want to create an anchor chart entitled *Tips for Reading Informational Texts*, and include these tips:

- Look at the visual information—photographs, illustrations, and more!
- Wonder about the topic.
- Pick a starting point—use the table of contents, headings, or index to help you.
- Read to answer a question.

(Adapted from Making It Real: Strategies for Success With Informational Texts *[Hoyt, 2002, p. 5])*

Ask Thought-Provoking Questions

TARGET

I can ponder and use evidence from the text or illustrations to answer questions and share my thinking.

PREPARATION

Select a literary or informational picture book that will generate discussion. For a sampling of some of my favorite picture books along with accompanying thought-provoking questions and ideas for discussion see the Comprehension Conversation Parent Notes in the online resources (page 160).

EXPLANATION

Thought-provoking questions have more than one right answer. They prompt students to integrate various aspects of the story or several pieces of information together to come to a bigger understanding. When questions of this type are paired with collaborative conversations, they elevate the thinking in the classroom because students are constantly articulating and clarifying their thoughts.

EXPERIENCE

Here I've listed some "generic" thought-provoking questions that will guide students to a deeper understanding about the texts they're hearing and reading. As a reminder, you might consider making a copy of the questions to post near your read-aloud chair.

FICTION	INFORMATIONAL	FOLLOW-UP QUESTIONS
• What does this title tell you about this book? • Notice the look on [the character's] face. How do you think he or she is feeling? • Why do you think [the character] reacted the way he or she did? What makes you say that? • How is the main character like you or different from you? • How are [the character] and [another known character] similar? • What do you think caused [the event] to happen? • Were you satisfied with the ending? If not, how would you choose to end this story?	• What are you wondering about this topic? • What questions do you have before we start reading? • What do you think this author is trying to teach you? How do you know? • What else did you learn? • What was the most important part? Why do you think that? • What was the most interesting part? Why? • What did you notice about the visual images the author used to help us as readers? • How has the author chosen to organize the information?	• Why do you think I'm asking you this question? • Tell me more about your thinking. • Who has another idea? • Who can add to that idea or work with it in a different way? • Can you push back against that thinking? What's another way to look at that? • How can you take what you learned from reading this book and apply it to your own life? • Do you have any lingering questions? How might you go about answering them?

(Adapted from Taberski, 2011, p. 103; Johnston, 2012)

Transforming Literacy Teaching in the Era of Higher Standards, K–2 © 2015 by Maria P. Walther, Scholastic Teaching Resources

Big Idea: Make Thinking Visible

Thinking. I believe it is the essence of the Common Core and the goal of all our teaching. But thoughts are invisible, and unless we write them down, they come and go quickly. Two ways we can make thought processes visible for students are thinking aloud and creating anchor charts. Thinking aloud is a powerful way to plant the metacognitive talk and habits of proficient readers and writers in the minds of our youngest learners. Then, anchor charts provide a place to record thinking or other habits of mind for learners to reference at a later date.

Think Aloud

TARGET

I can listen carefully to the thinking of others.

PREPARATION

If thinking aloud is new to you, it is helpful to annotate or mark certain places in the text that you want to stop and make a teaching point.

EXPLANATION

Thinking aloud is just one of the many ways we provide mentor or expert support to our young readers and writers. For readers, "[w]hen teachers think aloud, sharing their thinking as they read, the mysterious process of understanding becomes visible for children. Children learn to awaken the 'voice in their minds' so that reading becomes an active process in which they have an ongoing, inner conversation with themselves and the text" (Keene & Zimmerman, 2013, p. 604). The same holds true for writers. If we think aloud as we demonstrate our writing, we let our students know that writing doesn't magically happen. Instead, it is a complex thinking process that even adults find challenging.

EXPERIENCE

Begin by setting the parameters for think-aloud experiences in your classroom. Explain to students that you will be asking yourself questions and then answering them to let students peek into your brain. Young children have a difficult time being patient during a think-aloud and want to answer your questions. So it is wise to devise some kind of signal, visual or verbal, to indicate when you are thinking aloud. Some teachers wear a "thinking cap," others hold a thinking bubble above their head.

Snippet of a Think-Aloud Experience Using *Bully* (Seeger, 2013)

Today I'm going to think aloud while I'm reading the book *Bully* by Laura Vaccaro Seeger. I might ask myself questions and then answer my own questions so you can hear my thinking. If I need your help or want you to share your thinking, I'll let you know.

- [*Page before Title Page*]: Wow! I can tell by the look on the brown bull's face that his feelings are hurt because the gray bull said "GO AWAY!"

- [*Title Page*]: The title is *Bully*. When I first looked at the cover [turn back to the cover, point to the brown bull and the title] I thought the brown bull was going to be the bully, but after reading the first page, I'm not sure. I guess I'll have to keep reading to find out.

- [*Next six two-page spreads*]: Hmmmm! I guess I was right after all. Brown Bull is not being very nice to the other animals. Wait! I want to go back and reread these pages. [Reread]: I noticed that every time Brown

Bull says something unkind to his friends, he gets bigger and bigger. I wonder why Laura Vaccaro Seeger did this? Perhaps it is because bullies feel more important when they are making someone else feel sad.

- [*Next page*]: I'm so happy that the goat stood up to the bully. I wonder what is going to happen next?

Create Anchor Charts

TARGET

When I want to locate information about something we learned, I know right where to find it.

PREPARATION

Gather materials to record students thinking. I prefer 18- x 24-inch sheets of white drawing paper (found in school supply catalogs) rather than lined chart paper. The white drawing paper is less expensive, smaller, and easier to hang around the room. I also use colorful markers because using different colors on charts helps learners quickly find the information when you refer to the chart. If your space is limited, you can create charts electronically and have students store them in a file for easy access, or take photos of charts for students to keep in a reference notebook or binder.

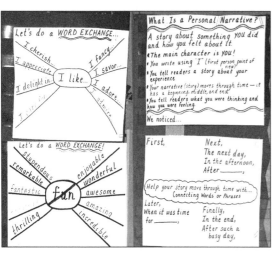

Display anchor charts in your room.

EXPLANATION

If you were to visit my classroom in August, you would notice that there is basically nothing hanging on the walls. There are the necessary reference tools—an alphabet, the blank word wall, and a number line. But other than that, you would see a lot of empty space. If you were to return in May, however, you'd see a much different view. Anchor charts and other evidence of student learning hang from the walls (and even the ceiling). This transformation occurs slowly, as I gather my students' thinking and post it on charts that we reference throughout the year.

EXPERIENCE

- Determine a purpose for the anchor chart.
- Record students' thoughts and ideas along with their names to honor their contribution to the chart. I usually quickly jot down their ideas on a sticky note or in my notebook, then later transfer them to the chart. For younger students, it's helpful to add simple drawings, icons, or other visuals to guide their understanding of the text.
- Display the chart in the room and take a photo of it so you remember it for next year!

Big Idea: Integrate Foundational and Language Skills

Foundational and language standards do not exist in a vacuum. Our young learners need to develop these skills and strategies so they can effectively comprehend text and communicate with others. As you've already learned, the intentional teaching of the foundational and language skills is woven throughout the day and developed in both the reading and writing workshops. The two main instructional contexts where direct teaching of these skills takes place are during the morning message and in mini-lessons.

Introduce, Revisit, or Review Concepts Using the Morning Messages

TARGET

Learning targets vary based on the foundational or language skill that is the focus of the message. Messages may also have multiple learning targets. For example, in one message (see sample below) you could target these skills:

- Understand the question words *who, what, where, when, why,* and *how.*
- Recognize and name ending punctuation.
- Recognize and read sight words.

For menus of morning messages tied to foundational and language skills, see *Month-by-Month Trait-Based Writing Instruction* (Walther & Phillips, 2009) and *Month-by-Month Reading Instruction for the Differentiated Classroom* (Walther & Phillips, 2012).

PREPARATION

Create a space for students to gather to read and interact with the message. It could be in front of your chalkboard, whiteboard, chart paper, interactive whiteboard, or document camera.

EXPLANATION

The morning message is one of the best ways I've found to authentically integrate foundational and language skills into my daily instruction. Based on my students' learning needs, I use messages to quickly introduce, revisit, or review foundational and language skills. The beauty of the morning message is that it takes only five to ten minutes of instructional time each day—but when you multiply the minutes by the total number of school days, it adds up to an abundant amount of time demonstrating, talking, and thinking about writing.

> **MORNING MESSAGE SAMPLE**
>
> How are all of these sentences alike?
>
> * Who went out to play?
> * Where did you play?
> * What did you do?
> * When did you go home?

Create a space for students to gather to read and interact with the morning message.

EXPERIENCE

The steps to a morning message experience are as follows:

1. Determine your learning target(s) for the message.

2. Based on the learning target(s), decide whether you'll write the message yourself, or write it with your students in a shared or interactive format, or invite students to write the message themselves. For the sample message above, I would write the message to my students before they arrived.

3. After the message is composed, using a pointer or your finger, point to the words as you chorally read the message. This is a helpful way to reinforce the concepts of print.

4. To complete, revise, or edit the message, invite students to step up to the message to help. You may want to have a small container of chalk or markers handy for easy access. To increase participation, set the guideline that each student only gets one opportunity per day to assist at the board. Others can answer questions as you discuss and make teaching points. Vary students from day to day so all learners get frequent chances to participate. The discussion surrounding the sample message would sound like this:

- What did you notice about the sentences? [*Student notices the question marks.*]
- Can someone come up and circle a question mark? [*Ask the following questions as different students are coming up to circle the question marks.*]
  - Where are all the question marks? What does a question mark signal? How does it sound when we read a question? [*Chorally reread questions.*]
- What else do you notice? [*Student notices the first words all start with a* w.]
- I agree. Do you notice anything else about these words? [*Student notices they all have* wh.]

5. Once the message is complete, *reread* with fluency and expression and recap the new learning related to the target(s).

Weave Concepts Into Reading and Writing Mini-Lessons

TARGET

Learning target(s) vary based on the foundational or language skill that is the focus of the mini-lesson.

PREPARATION

Create a space where students can gather to read and interact with the text you've chosen as the focus of the mini-lesson. It could be on the chalkboard, whiteboard, chart paper, interactive whiteboard, or document camera.

EXPLANATION

Mini-lessons for teaching foundational and language skills have the following characteristics:

- *Short*—They last only about 7–10 minutes.
- *Focused*—You can't teach everything in one mini-lesson, so stick to your selected learning target(s). Your mini-lesson can either be an introduction or review of a particular foundational or language skill or strategy.
- *Aligned*—The standards provide the end-of-year expectations for students. There are prerequisite skills, concepts, and understandings that students must develop in order to meet the standard. Mini-lessons provide time to teach those prerequisites. See Planning Guides in the online resources (page 160) for a detailed list of the underlying concepts related to the Language Standards.
- *Needs Based*—You know your students better than anyone. Use the information you gather from your observations, conferences, and formative assessments to determine the content of your mini-lessons.

EXPERIENCE

As you develop mini-lessons to teach foundational and language skills, keep these tips in mind:

- Anchor your mini-lesson in a piece of text that you've read at a *different* time—you won't have time to read aloud and complete a mini-lesson in 7–10 minutes.
- Design lessons that encourage student interaction and accountable talk.
- *Recommend* rather than require that students apply what you've introduced in their reading or writing.
- Remember that young children need multiple exposures over time before they will be able to transfer a skill or strategy to their reading or writing. Provide these by revisiting mini-lessons

Transforming Literacy Teaching in the Era of Higher Standards, K–2 © 2015 by Maria P. Walther, Scholastic Teaching Resources

over the course of the year and re-teaching the same mini-lesson in small groups to students who need additional exposure.

Big Idea: Spotlight Vivid Vocabulary

The next two teaching routines offer ongoing opportunities to spotlight and teach vocabulary in the meaningful contexts of poems and picture books. In these routines, students are actively involved in discussing, elaborating on, and demonstrating meanings of newly learned words. This kind of embedded word learning enhances learners' ability to infer word meanings so they can better comprehend what they're reading. As a result, these skilled comprehenders are more adept at figuring out the meaning of unknown words from context. So the process becomes a cycle of success for your students.

Unleash the Power of Poetry

TARGETS

- I can find feeling words or phrases in a poem or story.
- I can find sensory words or phrases in a poem or story.
- I can find words that make a poem or story have rhythm.
- I can ponder the meaning of the words in a poem, story, or song.

PREPARATION

- Collect or compile poems that match your students' interests and are related to curricular topics, seasons, holidays, and more.
- Display a poem where all of your learners can see it.
- Reproduce the poem for individual students' poetry notebooks (a 3-ring binder where students store the poems and songs they've learned throughout the year).

EXPLANATION

In our book, *Teaching Struggling Readers With Poetry* (2010), Carol Fuhler and I outlined eight reasons why poems are perfect for all readers—and essential for struggling readers. For the purpose of this experience, let's focus on three of these reasons:

- Poetry plays with language.
- Poems are comprised of well-chosen words.
- Poetry contains rich vocabulary.

Noticing and Naming Poetic Elements

Here are some poetic elements that you and your students will discover in poetry.

* **Rhythm**—Poets use rhythm to emphasize specific words, suggest movement, or create mood. Rhythm also makes poetry enticing for children to read, recite, or move to its beat!

* **Rhyme**—Gives poems their musical quality.

* **Repetition**—Repeated words or phrases emphasize meaning, create rhythm, or sometimes work together to make sound effects.

* **Alliteration**—Is the repetition of the beginning consonant.

* **Onomatopoeia**—Words that make a sound like the action represented by the word help reader make a mental image.

* **Sensory images**—These images appeal to one of the five senses and help readers make pictures in their mind.

* **Simile**—Is a comparison using *like* or *as*.

* **Metaphor**—Is a comparison in which one object or idea is said to *be* another object or idea.

* **Personification**—Refers to inanimate objects and animals as if they were people.

* **Creative conventions**—Make use of dashes, italics, and fonts of different sizes, shapes, and colors for emphasis.

A Few of My Favorite Poetry Books

Forest Has a Song (VanDerwater, 2013)	A girl describes the sights and sounds of the forest in this collection of nature poems.
Ode to a Commode: Concrete Poems (Cleary, 2015)	A clever collection of concrete poems about everything from toilets to Christmas trees. Includes an explanation of concrete poems and idea starters.
Poem-mobiles: Crazy Car Poems (Lewis & Florian, 2014)	A collection of 22 poems about inventive and unusual cars including "Hot Dog Car" and "The Dragonwagon."

EXPERIENCE

- Display the poem in a place where all children can see and interact with it.
- Read the entire poem aloud with phrasing and expression.
- Reread the poem line by line and invite students to be your echo by repeating each line the same way you read it.
- As a class, chorally read the entire poem.
- Revisit the poem to notice and discuss key words, phrases, or figurative language. See chart on page 95 for a description of poetic elements.

Embed Vocabulary Instruction

TARGETS

- I can think about what words mean.
- I can learn the meaning of new words.
- I can make real life connections between words and how they are used.

PREPARATION

Select three target words from a text you plan to read aloud. Write a kid-friendly definition for each word. It is helpful to embed an example in your definition. See the chart on page 97 for some exemplar texts, along with words and kid-friendly definitions. When selecting words from a read-aloud text, ask yourself the following questions:

- Is the concept represented by this word understandable to your students? Does the word relate to other words or concepts children have been studying? Think about the standards—look for verbs with shades of meaning or closely related adjectives, for example, words like *fuming* (being very mad), *pounce* (jump quickly), or *filthy* (being very dirty). Does the word contribute to the text or situation?
- Is the meaning of the word easy enough to explain?
- Does the word have extensive possibilities for use? Is it a word students will encounter in other texts? Will they use it when they speak or write (Beck, McKeown, & Kucan, 2013, p. 37–39)?

Transforming Literacy Teaching in the Era of Higher Standards, K–2 © 2015 by Maria P. Walther, Scholastic Teaching Resources

Read-Alouds With Rich Vocabulary

City Cat (Banks, 2013) A city cat stows away with a family on a European vacation, and then, using various modes of transportation, follows them on their travels.		*beckoning*: pulling someone toward something or signaling someone to come with you *pounces*: jumps quickly in order to get something, like a lion pounces on its prey *squints*: partly closing the eyes, like you have to do on a sunny day
The Dandelion's Tale (Sheehan, 2014)— Dandelion has one wish, to be remembered. So, before her seedpods blow away, she tells her stories to Sparrow. After a storm blows all her seedpods away, Sparrow remembers Dandelion and tells her tales to her children.		*dilemma*: a time when you have to choose between two actions and neither will be a good solution. Like Dandelion's dilemma— she knows she is going to lose her seedpods, but she can't go anywhere because she is stuck in the ground. *envious*: to want something that someone else has. You might be envious of your sister or brother when they get a new toy and you do not get one. *recalled*: remembered a past event, like when you recall your last birthday party.
Peanut Butter and Jellyfish (Krosoczka, 2014)—Best friends, Peanut Butter and Jellyfish, are endlessly taunted by Crabby. One day, Crabby gets caught in a lobster trap. When the duo set him free, he apologizes for his behavior and they all become friends.		*budge*: to move or begin to move to a new place. Sometimes my dog won't budge when he is sitting in a sunny spot. *relentless*: doing something without stopping or thinking about other people's feelings, like a bully who is relentless and keeps saying mean things to a child over and over. *taunt*: to make fun of or tease someone, like when a bully taunts someone by calling them names.

EXPLANATION

In their book *Bringing Words to Life: Robust Vocabulary Instruction*, Isabel Beck and her colleagues (2013) share a framework for embedded vocabulary instruction for young learners. Embedded vocabulary instruction is defined as teaching vocabulary using the texts you're sharing during your read-aloud experiences.

EXPERIENCE

Beck and her colleagues suggest that the following teaching sequence take place after the read-aloud has been completed:

1. Connect the word back to the book.

2. Invite learners to say the word.

3. Provide a kid-friendly definition.

4. Share real-life examples/connections to the word by relating it to familiar places or things your students do, like, or are interested in.

5. Engage in conversations to help students interact with the target words in different ways:
   - Providing their own examples or sentences. (A lion *pounces*. What are other creatures that *pounce*?)
   - Showing how something might look or act. (Show me what it looks like to *pounce*.)
   - Making a choice about the use of words and explaining why they made that choice. (When might a lion *pounce*—when it sees its prey or when it sees a flower? Why?).

6. Invite learners to say the word again.

Chapter 6

Inquiry Experiences— Reading in Focus

Although the inquiry experiences in the next two chapters are grouped as "Reading in Focus" and "Writing in Focus," they continue to integrate the language arts in meaningful ways. Throughout these inquiry experiences you will find opportunities to strengthen children's ability to read, write, listen, converse, think, wonder, discover, and apply new learning. Each experience, when repeated over time throughout the year, is designed to move students toward independence. To do this, think about the stages of inquiry and stages of the gradual release model. On page 99, I've synthesized these stages. It is important to note that the stages are not linear and that students, with your support, may need to move back and forth between the stages to deepen their understanding. Samantha Bennett (2007) and Debbie Miller (2013a) describe this as the "catch and release" model rather than the gradual release model. Some reasons you might want to "catch" learners include:

Go online to view a video on Inquiry Experiences— Reading in Action; see page 160.

- To publicly affirm a child's thinking or work while sharing strategies for others. "I noticed that Noah has developed a lot a questions during his investigation. Noah, can you tell us how you went about that?"

- To transition to another task. "Now that you've had time to research

Transforming Literacy Teaching in the Era of Higher Standards, K–2 © 2015 by Maria P. Walther, Scholastic Teaching Resources

spiders with your research team, join me for read aloud to find out what Nic Bishop's book can add to your learning."

- To refocus when learners are confused. "I'm noticing that some of you are having difficulty gathering sources; let's join in the conversation circle to brainstorm some strategies."

If you take time to observe and listen carefully to your students, they will teach you everything you need to know as you strive to make these inquiry experiences relevant to your learners and your teaching context.

Stages of Inquiry (Harvey and Daniels, 2009)	Stages of Gradual Release (Pearson and Gallagher, 1983)
IMMERSE • Invite curiosity • Build background • Find topics • Wonder	**TEACHER MODELING AND DEMONSTRATION** • Read aloud • Think aloud • Demonstration writing • Scaffolded conversations
INVESTIGATE • Develop questions • Search for information • Discover answers	**GUIDED PRACTICE** • Shared and interactive reading and writing • Guided reading and writing • Partner reading and writing • Individual reading and writing conferences
COALESCE • Intensify research • Synthesize information • Build knowledge	**SUPPORTED "INDEPENDENT" PRACTICE** • "Independent" reading and writing with conferring
GO PUBLIC • Share learning • Demonstrate understanding • Take action	**APPLICATION IN AUTHENTIC CONTEXTS** • Share learning • Demonstrate understanding • Take action

A Common Sense View of Gradual Release

Ongoing Assessment and Celebration

TEACHER MODELING AND DEMONSTRATION "I Show You"	SHARED DEMONSTRATION "We Do It"
GUIDED PRACTICE WITH DESCRIPTIVE FEEDBACK "You Try It"	INDEPENDENT APPLICATION "You Apply It"

Adapted from: Pearson & Gallagher, 1983; Miller, 2013; Routman, 2008

Big Idea: Read! (and Read Some More!)

TRANSFORMING TEACHING	
Everyone, including the teacher, reads during D. E. A. R. (Drop Everything and Read) or S. S. R. (Sustained Silent Reading).	Teachers surround "independent" reading by actively structuring conditions, such as explicit instruction and teacher monitoring, to increase students' accountability and progress toward reading more complex texts.

I chose to begin this chapter with the end in mind. Our ultimate goal is to have students apply their accumulated knowledge from all their learning experiences to any text they read. Next, I'll share an inquiry experience specifically designed to support students as they strive to become proficient, independent readers.

Inquiry Experience: Read Just-Right Books

Teach readers how to find just-right books.

Professional Books That Have Helped Shape My Independent Reading Time

❋ *The Reading Zone* (Atwell, 2007)

❋ *Month-by-Month Reading Instruction for the Differentiated Classroom* (Walther & Phillips, 2012)

❋ *No More Independent Reading Without Support* (Miller & Moss, 2013)

❋ *Reading With Meaning* (Miller, 2013b)

❋ *The Daily Five: Fostering Literacy Independence in the Elementary Grades* (Boushey & Moser, 2014)

TARGETS

I can read just-right books for longer and longer amounts of time each day.

PREPARATION

- Guide students as they gather a collection of "just-right" books. A just-right book has the following characteristics:
  - Child can read it with 98% accuracy or higher
  - Reader comprehends what he or she is reading
  - Book matches child's interests

  In order to put book after book in the hands of young readers, primary classrooms have to have *a lot* of books. Richard Allington suggests that a well-stocked classroom library includes at least 500 *different* book titles and notes that the exemplary teachers he observed had collections in the 1,500-book range (Allington, 2006). Obviously, an emergent reader who is reading at Levels A–C (Fountas & Pinnell, 2009) will need a lot more books than a fluent reader reading at Level M and above. So, the lower the grade level you teach, the more books you will need.

- Think about how you want to organize your students during independent reading. I divide my class into two groups, Then, each day, I simply alternate between Group 1— students reading in a "pillow place" or on the floor—and Group 2— students reading in a "desk place." Then they switch. To keep track, I move a clothespin back and forth between the words "Group 1" and "Group 2"—simple! (Walther & Phillips, 2012).

EXPLANATION

The mantra students hear in my classroom is, "The more you read, the better you get!" To meet Standard 10, research and common sense tell us that primary-grade children have to begin by reading texts they can read and *want* to read. In fact, "it is the better readers in U. S. classrooms who daily engage in much high-success reading activity (98% accuracy or higher) and who develop into our good readers" (Allington, 2013, pp. 524–525). If we know that access to a wide range of texts and intrinsic motivation are the keys to voluminous high-success reading, then matching students to texts is the first step to helping them develop lifelong reading habits. When offered a steady diet of successful reading experiences, along with your expert scaffolding and support to read increasingly complex texts, children will inch toward the level of complexity recommended by the standards.

The second key to voluminous, high-success reading is a child's interest and intrinsic motivation. To me, this means children who love to read because it's enjoyable and who don't need extrinsic rewards like points, pizzas, or a purple-haired principal to motivate them to do it. Together, the characteristics of a classroom discussed in Chapter 1, and the tenets of a workshop approach highlighted in Chapters 3 and 4, create conditions where motivation flourishes. These research-proven characteristics of high-motivation classrooms are reviewed in the box at right.

EXPERIENCE

Demonstration

Starting on Day 1, I introduce, model, and then have students practice independent reading. During the demonstration, I explicitly show children what I expect of them during this time.

Guided Practice

I then provide students with a brief period to practice. I think it is important to leave students wanting more time. After they've had a few minutes to read independently, we debrief and problem solve.

Release Responsibility

Then, I assure students that they will have more time to read tomorrow! To increase students' stamina, I do the following:

- Review the purpose and importance of reading each day.
- Change the atmosphere in the classroom (dim the lights).
- **Slowly** increase independent reading time (add *less than a minute* each day).
- Model and remodel the expectations.
- Meet with small groups of students reading at lower levels to practice reading one book after another.
- Confer with reluctant and striving readers more frequently.
- Celebrate students who are building stamina and have them share their strategies.
- Share and celebrate—this provides a purpose for reading.

Introduce and display new books.

Characteristics of High-Motivation and High-Performing Classrooms

- ❋ Teacher does expressive read-alouds.

- ❋ Classroom is brimming with books at different levels.

- ❋ New books are regularly introduced and displayed throughout the classroom.

- ❋ Effort is emphasized when discussing student work.

- ❋ Learners are given choices in completion of their work.

- ❋ Students are engaged in authentic reading and writing experiences.

- ❋ Learning experiences promote higher-order thinking.

- ❋ Teacher uses small groups for instruction.

(Pressley, Dolezal, Raphael, Mohan, Roehrig, & Bogner, 2003)

Big Idea: Engage in Collaborative Conversations

TRANSFORMING TEACHING	
Teachers mainly lead the questioning and discussion.	Students mainly lead the questioning and discussion. They ask and answer questions not only about the key details in the text, but also about what others are thinking about the text to confirm or deepen their own understanding.

Collaborative conversations are the glue that cements the learning. Collaborative conversations are those in which students take the lead by asking and answering questions and expanding their knowledge by listening, responding, and reflecting on their peers' thoughts and ideas. Children who can orally express their ideas are better able to translate the same thoughts into written words. In the primary grades, the foundation of effective communication is built by fostering classroom time for accountable talk. In Sharon Taberski's book *Comprehension From the Ground Up* (2011), she wisely reminds us that "helping children comprehend text by boosting their oral language experiences should be among our top priorities" (p. 94). This sentiment is echoed in the Common Core State Standards for Listening and Speaking, giving yet another reason to slow down the pace and make time for children to talk with each other. How then do we nurture accountable talk among our students? The next two learning experiences will help to answer that question.

Inquiry Experience: Link My Thinking

TARGETS

- I can learn from my friends by listening carefully to what they say.
- I can think about what my friends are saying.
- I can link my thinking to my friends' thinking by asking questions or making comments.

PREPARATION

- Strategically pair students with a think-and-share partner. Consider partnering students who need support with language use or comprehension with students who are stronger in these skills.
- Make a chart with the "link your thinking" questions and comments, such as the one at left. (This chart and experience are adapted from Walther & Phillips, 2012, p. 52)
- Select a text to read aloud that will offer opportunities for students to turn and talk with their partner, practicing the questions and comments on the chart. For the demonstration below, I'll use the Caldecott Honor Book *Creepy Carrots* (Reynolds, 2012). Of course, you can use any book or digital media that matches your curriculum or learning targets.

> I can LINK MY THINKING by saying…
> Tell me more about your thinking
> I have the same thinking because…
> My thinking is different because…
>
> I can LINK MY THINKING by asking…
> What do you think?
> Why do you think that?
> Did you notice…?

Nurture accountable talk among students.

EXPLANATION

It is through collaborative conversations that students' learning grows. Explicitly teaching children the language they can use to "link their thinking" with a partner's thinking will help them move toward independence and come to understand that the more they listen to their peers, the smarter they get. This is a challenging concept for egocentric young learners, especially those who like to be "right" all the time or those who always have their hand up and only want to share their thinking with the whole class. Be patient; the more you expect children to talk with a partner, the less they will feel the need to share everything with you. This small yet powerful instructional shift is one of the keys to fostering independent learners.

EXPERIENCE

Demonstration

Demonstrate with another teacher (or a student) what a collaborative conversation sounds like, purposefully using the questions and comments on the chart and doing the following:

- Show the cover of the book *Creepy Carrots* (Reynolds, 2012) or another text and ask, "What do you think this book might be about?"

- Begin your demonstration by showing a "typical" turn-and-talk conversation during which both you and your partner talk at the same time. Then ask the class "What did you notice?" [We couldn't hear anything with both people talking.]

- Next, show how to link your thinking by saying something like this:

Teacher: What do you think this book is about?

Partner: I think it is about carrots who scare a rabbit.

Teacher: Why do you think that?

Partner: The carrots on the cover have mean faces, and the title is *Creepy Carrots*. What do you think?

Teacher: I have the same thinking as you.

Partner: Did you notice the only color Peter Brown used on the cover was orange? I wonder why he did that?

Teacher: Maybe because the book is about carrots.

Partner: Thanks for thinking with me!

Teacher: You're welcome.

Guided Practice

Continue reading the text and begin to release responsibility. Pause and ask students to turn to their think-and-share partner and see if they can figure out the answer to your question together. Circulate among the students to prompt and scaffold during their conversation. Remind them to see how many times they can link their thinking by using the comments and questions on the chart. Wrap up the experience by asking students to share how thinking with a partner helped their learning grow.

Release Responsibility

Continue this experience throughout the year. Partner conversations can occur during read aloud, guided reading, content-area studies, or any time you want students to think together about a book or topic. You will need to demonstrate and practice many, many times before students are able to do this well on their own. In addition, I usually review the anchor chart after long weekends or other breaks from school. Here are a few tips to help keep collaborative conversations engaging and active:

- Teach students that if their usual think-and-share partner is absent, they simply join the pair behind them.

- Periodically switch think-and-share partners.

- Remember that you do not have to ask a few children to share with the whole class after they've talked with their partner. This not only saves time, but it also creates a culture where students' one-on-one conversations are valued as much as those they have with you during whole-class discussions.

Inquiry Experience: Converse With Friends

TARGETS

- I can learn from my friends by listening carefully to what they say.

- I can think about what my friends are saying.

- I can link my thinking to my friends' thinking by asking questions or making comments.

PREPARATION

- Create a space in your classroom where children can sit in a circle (or an oval if your room is small like mine!).

- Define this arrangement for students. I call this our "conversation circle" so that students know that when we're sitting is this space our agreed-upon norms for discussion will be different from when we are sitting "story style," as Debbie Miller (2013b) calls it or in our "places for learning" (Walther & Phillips, 2012).

- Select a text or topic that will spark varying opinions. I've found that historical fiction titles work well for conversation circles and as an added bonus, historical fiction "builds background, illuminates past events, and poses possibilities for future problem solving" (Fuhler & Walther, 2007, p. 150).

EXPLANATION

Whole-class conversations not only build students' ability to converse with and learn from their peers, but they also strengthen your classroom community. Once you have the norms for the conversation circle established, you can use this forum to problem solve issues that arise on the playground or in the classroom, to make whole-class decisions, or simply to share weekend happenings. The possibilities are endless!

EXPERIENCE

Demonstration and Guided Practice: Introducing the Conversation Circle

To get students used to sitting and conversing in a circle, at the beginning of the year you might do the following community-building activity, found in the book *Bullying Hurts: Teaching Kindness Through Read Alouds and Guided Conversations* (Laminack & Wadsworth, 2012, p. 137).

- Sit in your conversation circle.

- Hold a beanbag in your hand. Look at a child and say, "Hi, my name is [state your name]. What's your name?"

- Toss the beanbag to that child. Then he or she makes eye contact with another child and repeats the introduction.

- Continue this way until each child has been introduced.

- During the first few weeks of school, you can repeat the introductory experience by asking different questions.

  - I'm [state your name] and I love [state favorite food]. What's your favorite food?

  - I'm [state your name] and I'm learning how to [state something you're learning how to do]. What are you learning how to do?

  - I'm [state your name] and I like to read [state favorite kind of book]. What's your favorite kind of book?

Release Responsibility: Creating Norms and Cultivating Conversations

When you observe that students understand how to sit and take turns in the conversation circle, you are ready to release responsibility.

- Think about how you want to facilitate collaborative whole-group or small-group conversations. I've listed my norms and some of the thinking behind them in the box at right.

- After reading a thought-provoking book, invite students to sit in the conversation circle and pose a question. Some questions I use when we're first starting out are:

  - What was your opinion of the book and why?

  - Were you satisfied with the ending of the book? Why or why not?

- Once you've had a few conversations, collaborate with your students to create a chart of agreed-upon norms for discussion.

- Adjust norms as you turn over more and more responsibility throughout the year.

When We Are Sitting in Our Conversation Circle We Will . . .

❋ Listen carefully and ponder the question. [*Note: I usually pose a text-dependent question.*]

❋ Raise our hands to begin the conversation. [*Note: Then, I select someone to begin the conversation by saying, "Anthony, would you like begin?"*]

❋ Listen carefully to the person who is talking.

❋ Think about what we want to add to his or her thinking.

❋ Say the person's name if we want to add something to his or her thinking or ask a question.

❋ Say, "You may go first" if two or more people begin talking at the same time.

❋ Give other people a chance once we've shared our thinking. [*Note: This helps to prevent one or two students from monopolizing a conversation.*]

❋ Invite people into the conversation by saying, "[*Name*], what do you think?"

Big Idea: Ask and Answer Questions About Key Ideas and Details Using Support From the Text

TRANSFORMING TEACHING	
• Ask questions that are not dependent on text- or illustration-based evidence for answers, like "Have you ever flown a kite?"	• Create text- or illustration-based questions that compel the reader to revisit the text, like "What was the problem with the kite? How do you know?"
• Primarily ask "one right answer" literal questions whose answers can easily be found in the text.	• Ask open-ended, higher-level questions to spark thoughtful debate and collaborative conversations that lead to deep understanding of the text.
• Read informational texts once to learn about the main idea and details.	• Select excerpts of texts to read closely for a variety of reasons.

Inquiry Experience: Read Closely for Different Reasons

TARGETS

I can better understand the text by rereading and thinking carefully about the words and pictures or visuals.

PREPARATION

Select a text and identify a few parts or passages to closely read. Then, create text- or illustration-dependent questions. This preparation is a lot more productive if you do it with your colleagues. In fact, selecting texts for close reading and crafting text-dependent questions is a meaningful professional learning activity. Once the questions are created, tuck them inside the front of your book; that way they will be there when you need them! See the box on page 107 for types of text-dependent questions. I've also included a list of tried-and-true literary texts for close reading below.

Literary Texts for Close Reading

Going Places (Reynolds & Reynolds, 2014)	The "Going Places" contest is underway and Rafael wants to win. So he builds his go-cart to the exact specifications. Then he notices that Maya has taken a different approach. Together, they create their own unique vehicle.
Tough Boris (Fox, 1994)	This engaging text begs to be reread for many reasons. To begin, read to identify key details in both the words and illustrations (note that the story of the boy and his violin is only told through the illustrations). Reread to better understand the words Fox uses to describe Boris. Read again to notice the see-saw structure of the text. Finally, read closely to infer the big idea.

Types of Text- or Illustration-Dependent Questions for K–2 Listeners and Readers

To create text-dependent questions, preread the text and locate points in the text where you can ask engaging questions to prompt students to reread or reexamine the illustrations to discover the answers to the following question types (for specific examples, see charts on pages 107 and 108):

❋ **Sharing General Understandings:** Questions that ask students to share their general understandings allow them to retell a story or share the main ideas of an informational piece.

❋ **Identifying Key Details:** Key detail questions are found "right there" (Raphael, 1986) in the text and usually begin with *who, what, where, when, why,* and *how.*

❋ **Understanding Vocabulary:** Vocabulary queries guide readers to determine and clarify the meanings of unknown and multiple-meaning words, using word clues (affixes, root words), sentence-level context clues, or visual information. In addition, you can ask questions to prompt students to notice words in stories that suggest feelings or that appeal to the senses, or even discuss how words and phrases supply rhythm and meaning in a story, poem, or song.

❋ **Examining Text Structure:** With fiction, text-structure questions zoom in on the overall organization of a story and how it supports the readers' understanding. With informational text, these questions might ask readers to identify parts of the book, to know and use text features to find information, and to identify the main purpose of the text.

❋ **Determining Author's Purpose:** When determining the author's purpose, ask readers to identify whether the text was written to make them laugh (entertain), help them learn (inform), make them ponder, prompt them to do something (persuade), or for some other purpose. Notice the point of view the author chose to tell the story or share facts. Also, notice whose story is not being told.

❋ **Inferring Big Ideas:** Inferential questions prompt students to read between the lines.

❋ **Sharing Opinions:** Asking children to share their opinions about characters' actions, the author's choice of ending, and their preferences for one type of book over another will prompt them to use evidence from the text to support their stance.

❋ **Making Text-to-Text Connections:** Guide readers to consider how their understanding of one text helps them better understand a similar text.

Informational Texts for Close Reading

Snakes (Bishop, 2012)	Nic Bishop draws his readers into the world of snakes through stunning photographs and interesting, well-written information. I usually read his books a few pages at a time, like a chapter book, so we can enjoy the experience! Bishop's informational texts have earned him many awards and include the following titles: *Spiders, Frogs, Butterflies and Moths, Marsupials,* and *Lizards.*
Desert Elephants (Cowcher, 2011)	Closely read this book about the migration route of the desert elephants and the people who peacefully coexist with the elephants. Students can read multiple times to share general understandings, notice the chronological text structure, determine the author's purpose, and the big ideas.

EXPLANATION

In their article entitled "Close Reading in Elementary Schools," Douglas Fisher and Nancy Frey (2012) researched how to apply the practice of close reading to elementary classrooms. Close reading is when readers interact with the text by strategically reading and rereading to uncover deeper layers of meaning. Fisher and Frey suggest that as primary teachers our goals for close reading should be to demonstrate—through teacher modeling and interactive read aloud—how close reading works and to develop our own close reading habits. The aim for students is that they understand how to ask and answer questions to integrate information from the text into their existing background knowledge and to expand their schema. In a close reading experience, we limit our book introduction or pre-reading conversation so that we don't pre-answer the questions we want students to answer by carefully reading and rereading key portions of the text.

Close Reading— What Is It?

Close reading is one component of dynamic reading instruction where learners:

❋ Read strategically

❋ Interact with the text

❋ Reread to uncover layers of meaning that lead to deeper understanding

❋ Analyze multiple components of the text and illustrations

❋ Focus on the author's message

EXPERIENCE

Demonstration

After reading the text for enjoyment, ask text-dependent questions that encourage learners to reread or return to specific portions of the text. Demonstrate how rereading sentences, paragraphs, or reexamining the illustrations or visual information helps readers answer the questions. The questions that appear below are related to literary texts or stories. You will find text-dependent, close-reading questions for informational text on pages 110–111.

Literary Text-Dependent Questions

	Key Ideas and Details *(Ask these questions during the initial reading of the text.)*	Craft and Structure *(Ask these questions after at least one reading of the text.)*	Integration of Meaning and Ideas *(Ask these questions during a later reading of the text or while reading related texts.)*
QUESTION TYPE	• What does the text say?	• How does the text say it?	• What does the text mean? What is its value? How does it connect to other texts?
SHARING GENERAL UNDERSTANDINGS	• Can you retell the story?	• How did the author choose to organize this story? Let's read it again to figure that out!	• Why do you think the author chose this title for the text? Can you think of another title that would work?

 Transforming Literacy Teaching in the Era of Higher Standards, K–2 © 2015 by Maria P. Walther, Scholastic Teaching Resources

	Key Ideas and Details (*Ask these questions during the initial reading of the text.*)	Craft and Structure (*Ask these questions after at least one reading of the text.*)	Integration of Meaning and Ideas (*Ask these questions during a later reading of the text or while reading related texts.*)
IDENTIFYING KEY DETAILS	• Who is the main character? • What is the setting of this story? • Why do you think the character did _____?	• How does the author help you learn more about the main character and how he or she is feeling?	• What was the problem in the story? • How did the characters try to solve the problem? • Have you seen similar problems in other texts?
UNDERSTANDING VOCABULARY	• How does the author help us understand what the word _____ means? • The text says [literal interpretation]. What do you think the author really means? [Discuss figurative interpretation.]	• Why do you think the author chose to use this word here? Can you think of another word that might also work?	• When you come to a puzzling word, what do you do? Let's use the context of the sentences and the picture clues to try to figure out what this word means.
EXAMINING TEXT STRUCTURE	• How is this story organized? Are there clues to help you figure it out?	• Why do you think the author chose to organize this story in this way? • Are there any clues in the introduction, front flap, back blurb, or author's note?	• How does this structure help you better understand the text? • Can you think of another way the author might have done it?
DETERMINING AUTHOR'S PURPOSE	• Who is telling you this story? How do you know?	• Why do you think the author chose to use this point of view?	• Why do you think [author's name] wrote this piece? Does the book entertain or inform us? Show me how.
INFERRING BIG IDEAS	• Let's use the words and illustrations to infer what is going on right now in the text.	• Notice how the author doesn't tell you exactly [what is going on/how the character is feeling right now]. What clues help you figure it out? Let's reread!	• What is the big idea of this paragraph/passage/section? What in the text/illustration makes you say that?
SHARING OPINIONS	• In your opinion, did [the main character] change over time? Why do you think this?	• What is the author's opinion? How do you know that?	• Which did you prefer: [text 1] or [text 2]? Why?

	Key Ideas and Details *(Ask these questions during the initial reading of the text.)*	Craft and Structure *(Ask these questions after at least one reading of the text.)*	Integration of Meaning and Ideas *(Ask these questions during a later reading of the text or while reading related texts.)*
MAKING TEXT-TO-TEXT CONNECTIONS	• Does this text remind you of another text you've read or heard?	• Where do you think [the author] got the idea for this book? • Do you think [the author] read [a similar text] before he or she wrote this one?	• How did thinking about [a similar text] help you better understand this text? How does comparing and contrasting texts help you as a reader?

(Adapted from Fisher & Frey, 2012)

Release Responsibility

After introducing close reading and repeatedly practicing it with your whole class, continue to provide opportunities for students to closely read texts as you guide readers in small groups or individually during reading conferences. Remember that this instructional approach also works well with texts you are reading aloud in the content areas.

Informational Text-Dependent Questions

	Key Ideas and Details *(Ask these questions during the initial reading of the text.)*	Craft and Structure *(Ask these questions after at least one reading of the text.)*	Integration of Meaning and Ideas *(Ask these questions during a later reading of the text or while reading related texts.)*
QUESTION TYPE	• What does the text say?	• How does the text say it?	• What does the text mean? What is its value? How does it connect to other texts?
SHARING GENERAL UNDERSTANDINGS	• Can you recount the facts you've learned?	• How did the author choose to organize this informational text? Let's read it again to figure that out!	• Why do you think the author chose this title for the text? Can you think of another title that would also work?
IDENTIFYING KEY DETAILS	• What is the main thing the author is teaching you in this informational text? • Are there clues, like headings, to help us figure it out?	• What details does the author choose to give to support the main idea?	• How does this new information match with what you already know?

Transforming Literacy Teaching in the Era of Higher Standards, K–2 © 2015 by Maria P. Walther, Scholastic Teaching Resources

	Key Ideas and Details (Ask these questions during the initial reading of the text.)	Craft and Structure (Ask these questions after at least one reading of the text.)	Integration of Meaning and Ideas (Ask these questions during a later reading of the text or while reading related texts.)
UNDERSTANDING VOCABULARY	• How does the author show us that this word [show bold or colored word] is important? • How does the author help us understand what the word ____ means or is pronounced?	• Why do you think the author chose to use this word here? Can you think of another word that might also work?	• When you come to a puzzling word, what do you do? Let's reread to use the context of the sentences, visual cues, or glossary to try to figure out what this word means.
EXAMINING TEXT STRUCTURE	• How is this informational text organized? Are there clues to help you figure that out?	• Why do you think the author chose to organize this informational text in this way? • Are there any clues in the introduction, front flap, back blurb, or author's note?	• How does this structure help you better understand the text? • Can you think of another way the author might have done it?
DETERMINING AUTHOR'S PURPOSE	• Who is giving you the information? How do you know?	• Why do you think the author chose to use this point of view? • Where do you think the author got his or her facts? • What do you think he or she was trying to teach us?	• Why do you think [author's name] wrote this piece? Does the book entertain or inform us? Show me how.
INFERRING BIG IDEAS	• Let's use the words and illustrations to infer what is going on right now in the text.	• Notice how the author doesn't tell you exactly [what is going on]. What clues help you figure it out? Let's reread!	• What is the big idea of this paragraph/ passage/ section? What in the text/illustration makes you say that?
SHARING OPINIONS	• In your opinion, did the author teach you enough information? Is there more you would like to know?	• What is the author's opinion of this topic? How do you know that?	• Which did you prefer: [text 1] or [text 2]? Why?
MAKING TEXT-TO-TEXT CONNECTIONS	• Does this text remind you of another text you've read or heard?	• Where do you think [the author] got the idea for this book? • Do you think [the author] read [a similar text] before he or she wrote this one?	• How did thinking about [a similar text] help you better understand this text? How does comparing and contrasting texts help you as a reader?

(Adapted from Fisher & Frey, 2012)

Big Idea: Retell and Ponder Themes

TRANSFORMING TEACHING	
Students retell the basic elements of a story.	Students learn how to not only retell the basic elements of the story, but also infer the big idea or central message of the text.
Texts usually have familiar themes or central messages, such as friendship or telling the truth.	Select age-appropriate, read-aloud texts with less familiar and more challenging themes or central messages like homelessness, caring for the environment, bullying, and civil rights.

Inquiry Experience: Retell and Recount

TARGETS

Retelling a Story	Recounting Information
I can retell a story.	I can recount the main idea and key details that I've learned.
I know the elements (main parts) of a story.	I can figure out how a text was organized.

PREPARATION

To begin, pick texts for retelling that have a straightforward story structure with a clear beginning, middle, and end. As children get more skilled at retelling, select texts with more complex plot structures. Follow a similar progression with informational texts; start with texts that have a supportive organization, like descriptive texts about one clear topic. Then move to more complex nonfiction text structures, such as compare and contrast, sequence, cause and effect, or question and answer.

EXPLANATION

Retelling a story or recounting information in a nonfiction text is a useful way to help children summarize a story or determine important facts in an informational text. A child's retelling offers a window into his or her literal understanding of the text. This experience is the first step toward reaching the goal of retelling, along with inferring the theme or big idea. Once your students are adept at retelling, you'll transition to the next experience, where they'll learn to uncover themes.

EXPERIENCE

Demonstration and Guided Practice

Model each type of retelling and recounting explained here during a read-aloud, mini-lesson, or morning message. After your demonstrations, invite readers to join you in a shared retelling and retelling with partners.

Release Responsibility

To release responsibility to learners, prompt and coach readers as they practice retelling during guided reading or conferences. To assess whether they are able to retell independently, invite a child to retell one of his or her independent reading books.

Retelling a Story	Recounting Information
BEGINNING-MIDDLE-END Retell the story by describing what happened at the beginning, in the middle, and at the end.	**S. T. P.** (Stop, Think, Paraphrase) As students are reading a nonfiction text, invite them to *stop* after each page or paragraph (depending on the length of the text), *think* about what they just learned, cover the words, and using the picture or text feature, *paraphrase* their new learning. *(Adapted from Richardson, 2009)*
FIVE-FINGER RETELL Use the five-finger retell graphic found in the online resources (see page 160) to guide students as they retell a story.	**V. I. P.** (Very Important Points) To guide students in finding the main topic of a page or paragraph, provide them with one sticky-note strip. Students place the strip near the sentence that states the main topic. Remembering the V. I. P.s will help them to recount the main points. Once students are adept at pinpointing the main topic, provide them with two or three additional sticky-note strips in a different color to mark key details about the main topic. *(Hoyt, 2002, p. 189)*
SOMEBODY WANTED BUT SO Retell the story by stating the following: • Somebody: Character's name • Wanted: Character's goal or motivation • But: Problem(s) the character faces • So: How the character resolves the problem *(Macon, Bewell, & Vogt, 1991)*	**3-2-1 STRATEGY** After reading a paragraph or section, invite readers to share or jot down the following: • 3 Key details about the topic • 2 Questions they still have • 1 Main idea
C. L. A. P. S. Retell the story by stating the following: • Character: Character's name • Location: Setting • Action: Character's goal, what he or she wants to do or accomplish • Problem: Problem(s) the character faces • Solution: How the character resolves the problem *(Fuhler & Walther, 2007)*	**TEXT ANNOTATION** (Reading With a Pencil) Teach students how to do these annotation techniques on reproducible texts. They are ordered in complexity, so you can determine which makes sense for your grade level, or group of children. • Underline major points. • Circle key words or phrases that are confusing or unknown to you. • Write margin notes restating the author's idea. *(Fisher & Frey, 2012)*

Inquiry Experience: Uncover Themes

TARGET

I can infer the big idea or central message of a text.

PREPARATION

Select a text with a theme that matches your unit or essential understanding. Some books that work well for this learning experience are found in the chart below.

Each Kindness (Woodson, 2012) **Possible Theme:** Choose kindness.	Chloe learns a life lesson when her teacher does an activity that highlights the power of kindness. After this compelling lesson, Chloe wishes she had shown kindness to the new girl, Maya, instead of ignoring her because she was less fortunate and different. Unfortunately, Chloe never gets the chance to show kindness because Maya moves away.
Exclamation Mark (Rosenthal, 2013) **Possible Theme:** It's okay to be different.	Feeling alone in a world of periods, the exclamation mark tries everything to fit in and is about to give up when he meets the question mark. Question Mark helps him discover his unique talent: exclaiming!
Too Tall Houses (Marino, 2012) **Possible Theme:** We need each other; cooperate and work together.	Good friends and neighbors, Owl and Rabbit live in two small houses until they begin competing to make their houses taller and taller. When both houses are blown down, the two friends work together to build the perfect house.
Horsefly and Honeybee (Cecil, 2012) **Possible Theme:** We need each other; cooperate and work together.	A sweet story about a horsefly and honeybee that decide to nap in the same flower, have a fight, and each lose a wing. Later, when the bullfrog wants to eat them, they work together to fly away.

EXPLANATION

A well-written piece of children's literature engages and entertains the reader. The theme of a story quietly ties together the characters, setting, and plot and may reveal the author's purpose for writing the text. Guiding students as they uncover the theme leads to a deeper understanding of the text.

EXPERIENCE

Demonstration

After reading aloud a book with one or more clear themes, introduce the concept of theme by saying, "Today I'm going to use what I know about characters, their actions, and the events in this story to try

Transforming Literacy Teaching in the Era of Higher Standards, K–2 © 2015 by Maria P. Walther, Scholastic Teaching Resources

to figure out the theme. The theme of a story or poem is the big idea or message the author wants us to understand. Sometimes the author tells us the theme in the words, other times we have to infer it using clues." Continue by sharing your thinking about the theme(s) and the clues that led you to uncover it (or them).

Guided Practice

To help our young learners discover the theme(s) of a story, we can ask questions to scaffold the conversation as they begin this exploration. To draw learners' attention back into the text, use the follow-up question, "What evidence can you find in the text, illustrations, characters' actions, dialogue, or narration to support your thinking?" You might choose to mark those places in the text with a sticky note, so that you can revisit them during your conversation.

- What is the author trying to tell you that would make a difference in your life? How do you know that the author is telling you this?
- Has the main character changed over the course of the story? What caused these changes?
- What, if anything, has the main character learned?
- What was the conflict or problem? How was it resolved?
- Does the title or subtitle reveal the theme(s)?

A Sampling of Themes Found in Children's Literature

- ❈ Friendship is important.
- ❈ We need each other.
- ❈ Cooperate and work together.
- ❈ Stand up for yourself and others.
- ❈ Follow your heart.
- ❈ Solve problems.
- ❈ Choose kindness.
- ❈ It's okay to be different.
- ❈ Believe in yourself.
- ❈ Everyone grows up.
- ❈ There are ways to overcome fears.
- ❈ Greed and selfishness are bad.
- ❈ Kindness and generosity are good.
- ❈ The small or weak can overcome the powerful with wit and patience.

Release Responsibility

During guided, partner, or independent reading, provide students with a large sticky note to write down the theme and a few small sticky notes to mark the places in the book that helped them uncover that theme. Remind students that there can be more than one theme in a story. Invite them to bring their work to sharing time and teach the others how they determined the theme.

Big Idea: Describe Characters and Discover Connections

TRANSFORMING TEACHING	
The focus is on identifying character's traits.	Expand students' understanding of character by focusing on how a character's experiences and adventures impact the his or her decisions, and also how the character changes over time.
The focus is on identifying story elements	Extend the understanding of story elements to look at how characters respond to the events in a story.

Inquiry Experience: Notice Characters' Responses

TARGETS

- I can describe a character.
- I can notice how a character responds to events or other characters.
- I can notice how a character's experiences impact the character's feelings, actions, and decisions.
- I can notice how a character changes over time.
- I can use what I've learned from the character in my own life.

PREPARATION

- Select a book with one or more interesting multidimensional characters.
- Prepare a character study graphic organizer (see online resources, page 160) to match your learning target.

A Few of My Favorite Books for Character Study

Elena's Serenade (Geeslin, 2004)	Elena wants to be a glassblower but her papa says she can't because she's a girl. So, she dresses like a boy and heads to Monterrey to learn from the great glassblowers.
Emily's Blue Period (Daly, 2014)	Emily, an inspiring artist, is learning about Picasso. When her teacher asks her to make a collage of her home she is confused because she has two homes. In the end, she decides to make a heart-shaped collage showing "the home of her heart."
Those Shoes (Boelts, 2007)	Jeremy really wants "those shoes"—the pair of high-tops that everyone else has, but Grandma can't afford them. Later, Jeremy finds a pair in a thrift store that are much too small, but gets them anyway. After much debate, Jeremy ends up giving his too-small shoes to another boy in need.

EXPLANATION

Look back at the learning targets for this experience. They are ordered in complexity, beginning with the foundational skill of identifying character traits, then moving on to examining character's reactions, pondering a character's decisions, and finally, noticing how a character changes over time. For the first four learning targets, I've provided four different graphic organizers to guide your questions and conversations about characters (see online resources, page 160). When working to complete these graphic organizers with your students, note that authors reveal insights into a character in the following ways (this, by the way, would make a great anchor chart):

- Narration
- Conversation
- Illustrations
- Thoughts of the character
- Thoughts of other characters
- Actions

 Transforming Literacy Teaching in the Era of Higher Standards, K–2 © 2015 by Maria P. Walther, Scholastic Teaching Resources

For example, in the book *Clever Beatrice* (Willey, 2001), we learn about Beatrice's character in these ways:

- *Narration*: "Sure, she was little, but Beatrice loved riddles and tricks and she could think fast on her feet." "She walked over to where it lay on the ground and crouched over it, thinking hard."

- *Illustrations*: Beatrice is sitting at the table with her hand on her chin, thinking.

- *Thoughts of other characters*: "Sharp as a tack," her mother said.

- *Actions*: Beatrice outsmarts the giant.

EXPERIENCE

Demonstration and Guided Practice

As you are reading aloud, use a character study graphic organizer to help frame students' thinking about the character. Model how you use the clues the author gives you to learn more about the character. Then, for guided practice use the same graphic organizer when working with students individually or in a small group.

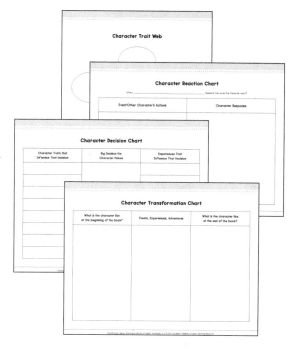

Release Responsibility

Once students are familiar with how to use one of the graphic organizers to learn more about the character, make copies and place them where students can access them. Encourage students to use the organizers as needed.

Inquiry Experience: Discover Connections in Nonfiction Books

TARGETS

- I can tell about the connections between events, ideas, or concepts in informational texts.

- I can show the connections by creating an illustration/diagram of the events.

- I can think about these connections when I'm researching and writing my own informational texts.

PREPARATION

- Gather information books that match your curriculum and that discuss or include diagrams or other features showing a chain of events, a timeline, a cycle diagram, and/or scientific method steps.

- Provide students with whiteboards, blank paper on a clipboard, or a digital device to create their own diagram.

EXPLANATION

To save time, I would suggest integrating this standards-focused learning experience into your science or social studies instruction so that the work children are doing is authentic and relevant. This inquiry experience begins by having children create their own graphic representation of the connection between events. Then, using the understanding gained from this experience, they are better able to discover, analyze, and understand the connections found in the informational texts they read.

EXPERIENCE

Demonstration and Guided Practice

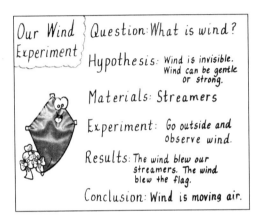

Work in a shared writing format to record steps in science experiment.

- During a content-area lesson, demonstrate how you would visually represent connected events you are studying. Discuss the connections between the events, how you show them with your drawing, and why thinking about how the parts are related helps you understand the whole process better.

- Engage in a shared inquiry with your students, such as interviewing a person about his or her life (timeline), watching a creature grow (life cycle), conducting a science experiment (scientific method steps), or charting the steps to putting on winter clothes.

- Throughout the inquiry process, work in a shared writing format to create a graphic representation to illustrate the connection between events.

Release Responsibility

While reading and discussing texts or engaging in other inquiry experiences that include connected events, invite students to draw their own visual representations of the connections.

Big Idea: Understand Vivid Vocabulary

TRANSFORMING TEACHING	
Specific vocabulary words are pre-taught.	Students ask and answer questions about words that are puzzling to them and think about why the author chose to use those particular words.
Vocabulary is taught by having children look up word meanings in a dictionary or glossary, copying the definition, and writing a sentence using that particular word.	Children make connections between words to learn new words and ideas.

Transforming Literacy Teaching in the Era of Higher Standards, K–2 © 2015 by Maria P. Walther, Scholastic Teaching Resources

Stories, poems, and songs with literal language are used.	Texts brimming with figurative language are used; students are invited to find words or phrases that evoke sensory images.
Students chorally read and chant songs and poems.	After chorally reading and chanting songs and poems, students think about how the author's word choices impact the rhythm of the song or poem.
Grammar instruction is sometimes viewed as a separate subject. Grammar, conventions, and editing are taught by asking students to fix incorrect examples.	Grammar instruction is embedded in reading and writing workshop so that students can directly apply what they are leaning to their own speaking and writing. Grammar, conventions, and editing are modeled by asking students to analyze well-crafted examples.

Inquiry Experience: Generate Word Webs

TARGETS

- I can ask and answer questions to figure out word meanings.
- I can make connections between new and known words.

PREPARATION

- Select a curriculum-related topic.
- Gather index cards or cut strips of paper for recording words.

EXPLANATION

When children are learning new vocabulary, it is important that they encounter words repeatedly in many contexts and actively process word meanings (Blachowicz & Fisher, 2000; Nagy & Townsend, 2012). Providing time for students to create word webs helps them process word meanings by connecting new words to known words and making connections between words (Blachowicz & Ogle, 2001). To make this experience go a bit more smoothly, demonstrate the process to your class once or twice before students try it in pairs or small groups. Keep in mind, that it's the process of sorting, categorizing, and mapping the words that's important. The finished product does not have to look beautiful or be something that you might hang on a bulletin board.

Support students as they sort words into categories.

EXPERIENCE

1. Invite students to brainstorm a list of words related to the topic.

2. Type or write each word on a separate "card." I make a table in a Word document and insert one word in each cell of the table.

3. Before cutting apart the cards, reproduce them so that students can sort words with partners or in small groups.

4. Support students as they sort words into categories. (You may choose to give them the categories or let them determine their own categories.)

5. Guide students as they use word cards to create a graphic organizer or visual representation of the connections between words and categories. An easy way to do this is to have children glue the words on a large piece of construction paper and use markers or crayons to draw lines and arrows.

6. Provide time for students to share their word webs and the thinking behind them with the class.

Inquiry Experience: Explore Words' Shades of Meaning

TARGETS

- I can choose the best verb for my sentence.
- I can choose the adjective that best describes the noun.

PREPARATION

Select books or mentor sentences from a particular book that will help you illuminate the following concepts:

- Verbs describing the same general action
- Adjective intensity
- Closely related verbs
- Closely related adjectives

EXPLANATION

As Jeff Anderson reminds us in his article "What Writing Is & Isn't" (2014), "Best practice in grammar lessons suggest that we focus on function and practical application" (p. 13). Anderson advocates that rather than showing children incorrect sentences to revise and edit, we should use mentor texts and mentor sentences from both published authors and student writers to show correct examples of the concept we are trying to teach. The inquiry experience that appears here is based on Anderson's four tenets for teaching grammar and conventions (Anderson, 2007, p. 3).

- Show powerful models rather than asking students to correct weak examples.
- Model your thought process and share writers' secrets rather than simply making corrections.
- Encourage experimentation and play rather than asking children to go on error hunts.
- Facilitate student thinking through grammar and mechanics choices rather than let them guess and hope for the best.

As with all the inquiry experiences, this experience is an exemplar lesson to use as a guide as you create your own experiences throughout the year.

EXPERIENCE

Show a powerful model

As an example, I'll use the book *Cheese Belongs to You!* (Deacon, 2013). After reading the first time for enjoyment, do the following:

Demonstration

Model a writer's thought process by thinking aloud: "I'm noticing how Alexis Deacon used adjectives in this story. She added one adjective after another to describe the rats. This helped me to know how many rats wanted the cheese. When she did this, she added a comma between the adjectives. Let's go back and look at that."

Guided Practice

Encourage experimentation by saying, "Let's think of another animal we could describe using a chain of adjectives." Provide time for students to orally share their animals and adjectives.

Release Responsibility

Facilitate children's thinking by asking, "When you're writing, how might you go about choosing adjectives to describe one of your characters? Do you think you could use an adjective chain? As a writer, why might you choose to do that? If you do that, what mark will you put between the adjectives?"

Big Idea: Notice Text Structures

TRANSFORMING TEACHING	
Students are asked to identify whether a text is fiction or nonfiction and/or to identify the characteristics of fiction and nonfiction texts.	Students identify and explain the differences between various types of text and the different ways authors approach the story or topic, with scaffolding as needed; then they apply these understandings to their own reading and writing.

Inquiry Experience: Read and Write Stories—Scene by Scene

TARGETS

- I can describe the overall structure of a story.
- I can tell how the beginning of a story introduces the action.
- I can tell how the ending of the story concludes the action.
- I can create my own story using scenes.

PREPARATION

- Collect mentor texts with descriptive beginnings and endings that clearly wrap up the action.
- Create your own story and draw or write each scene on a separate 5- x 7-inch index card

to create a storyboard. For a picture book with an example of storyboarding in it, look for *Patches Lost and Found* (Kroll, 2001).

- Get enough 5- x 7-inch index cards so each student can have three to five.

EXPLANATION

The most powerful way to help students understand the importance of story structure is by having them analyze structure in mentor texts, and then apply their understandings as they create their own story structure by storyboarding. I would suggest planning to do each stage of gradual release on a separate day or days. This will give you more time to surround each stage with rich conversations.

EXPERIENCE

Demonstration

Model telling your own story or retelling a picture book by creating a storyboard (drawing or writing one scene on each index card). Discuss the overall structure of the story, reviewing the elements of a story and how they work together.

Guided Practice

Invite students to order and reorder scenes from your storyboard in different ways. Use these questions to guide the conversation:

- Is it possible to tell this story in another way?
- Do you have to add additional scenes to make that work?
- What if the story started at the end? How would it change?

Release Responsibility

- Give learners index cards to draw and write the scenes of their own story or a story they have read or heard.
- Provide time for writers to tell (or retell) their story to a friend or to the class.
- Have index cards available during guided reading for retelling and during writing workshop in case students choose to make more storyboards.

Inquiry Experience: Identify New Learning From Informational Text Features

TARGETS

- I can notice and name text features.
- I can explain how text features help me learn new information.
- I can use text features in my own writing.

PREPARATION

- Gather engaging nonfiction texts that include a lot of visual features. Some of my favorite nonfiction series books include:

Transforming Literacy Teaching in the Era of Higher Standards, K–2 © 2015 by Maria P. Walther, Scholastic Teaching Resources

- Lightning Bolt Books (Lerner)
- Scholastic News Nonfiction Readers (Scholastic)
- Science Vocabulary Readers (Scholastic)
- ZooBooks Magazines
- Have sticky notes on hand

EXPLANATION

Students can glean extensive information by learning how to carefully "read" the visual features in nonfiction texts and thinking about what the author is trying to teach them. Over the course of the year, you might cover these and other features: photograph, diagram, close-up, map, graph, cross-section, and boldfaced or colored print.

EXPERIENCE

Demonstration

If you haven't already, introduce your students to the terms related to text features, a helpful resource is the *Introduction to Nonfiction Write-on/Wipe-off Flip Chart* (Charlesworth, 2009). I read a page or two of it a day, discuss the text feature and what information we learn from that feature, and then invite students to notice these features in the texts they're reading.

Once students are familiar with the features of nonfiction texts, you want them to think carefully about exactly what the feature is teaching or telling them. To do this, model the following procedure:

- Locate a feature in a familiar nonfiction book.
- Notice and discuss what you've learned from the feature as a reader.
- Jot down your new learning on a sticky note and place it next to the feature.

Release Responsibility

- Once students are familiar with this procedure, allow them to do it in pairs or groups of three.
- Invite students to share their new learning with their peers.
- Discuss how/why students might use text features in their own writing.

Big Idea: Consider Different Points of View

TRANSFORMING TEACHING	
Focus is on comprehending the story or content rather than considering point of view.	Students are guided to notice different aspects of story or text that will raise their awareness of point of view.

Inquiry Experience: Think About Points of View

TARGETS

- I can figure out who is telling the story at different points.
- I can notice who is telling the story or talking at different points in a story.
- I can read each character's words with a different voice when I read aloud.

PREPARATION

- Find any of the books in the Pinkerton series by Steven Kellogg. The first book in the series is *Pinkerton, Behave!* (Kellogg, 1979).
- Select books told from multiple points of view or those that offer the opportunity to discuss viewing the world from different perspectives. (See some examples in the box below.)
- Find books that students can read independently that contain dialogue between two characters, like the Elephant and Piggie books by Mo Willems or the You Read to Me, I'll Read to You books by Mary Ann Hoberman.
- Strategically pair students with a supportive reading partner.

Picture Books to Ponder Point of View

Picture a Tree (Reid, 2013)	Barbara Reid's unique Plasticine illustrations invite readers to notice that "there is more than one way to picture a tree."
Art & Max (Wiesner, 2010)	Arthur knows how to paint, and Max wants to learn. The color and font style change when each character speaks, making this an ideal book to discuss point of view.
One-Dog Sleigh (Casanova, 2013)	In the sequel to *One-Dog Canoe*, this cumulative, rhyming story follows a little girl and her perky dog as they pack one animal after another into their sleigh. Notice whether the girl or the animals are talking.
Winter Is For Snow (Neubecker, 2013)	A winter-loving brother is trying to convince his reluctant sister to join him outside for a fun-filled time in the snow. The text is written in two different colors, making it clear who is speaking at different points in the story. This book could also lead to opinion writing about winter!

EXPLANATION

I've read Steven Kellogg's Pinkerton books every year that I've been teaching first grade. It wasn't until I started thinking about helping my students better understand point of view, that I realized that Kellogg doesn't mark the dialogue in these books. Instead, the reader has to infer who is talking in order to better understand the story. Therefore, these books are ideal for helping readers develop an awareness of who is telling the story or talking at different points. For our youngest learners, an awareness of point of view begins by answering the question, "Who is telling this story?" It is helpful as you prepare for lessons on point of view that you are aware of the different types of point of view. (See the review on page 125.) I've started to note the type of point of view on the inside cover of the books I'm reading so I can intentionally ask questions that guide my learners to discover it on their own.

EXPERIENCE

Demonstration

Read a Pinkerton book to the class for fun and enjoyment.

The next day, during a second reading, tell listeners, "Today we are going to try to figure out or infer who is talking at different points in the story. You'll notice that Steven Kellogg does not tell us who is saying the words by writing 'said Mom,' like we've seen in other books. We have to look at the illustrations and think about what the words are saying to figure out/ infer whether it is the mom, the daughter, or another character in the story talking. Let's get started, reading detectives!" Show students how you use clues to figure out who is talking. Say, "This part is told from the girl's point of view, I can tell because . . ."

Guided Practice

- As you continue reading the story, guide students in figuring out who is talking and invite them to say the words as they think that character might say them.

- Discuss whether they have noticed alternating points of view in other books they've been reading. Invite children to share examples. Ponder how noticing who is talking helps them better understand the whole story.

- In your subsequent point-of-view experiences, select another book told from multiple points of view. While reading aloud, invite listeners to consider these questions:

  - How did the author choose to reveal the story?

  - Whose story is it?

  - Who is telling the story?

Release Responsibility

To practice reading aloud from different points of view, pair students and invite them to read a book told from two different points of view. Remind each partner to "become the character" by changing his or her voice. After the first reading, ask partners to switch parts. Continue to encourage this type of reading, when appropriate, during independent and guided reading.

Inquiry Experience: Learn From Images and Words in Informational Texts

TARGETS

- I can find information in the pictures and words.

- I can draw and/or write about my new learning.

A Quick Review of Different Types of Point of View

For your information, a quick review of the different types of point of view appears here:

❋ **Third-Person Omniscient:** This point of view ". . . allows the author complete freedom to crawl inside the skins of each of the characters, thinking their thoughts, speaking their words, and observing the action of the story. It also allows the author to speak directly to the reader . . ." (Kiefer, Hepler, & Hickman, 2007, p. 21).

❋ **Third-Person Limited Omniscient:** The story is told from one character's point of view. The reader learns what that character can see, hear, believe, feel, and understand.

❋ **First-Person:** The thoughts, experiences, and observations are told from the narrator's point of view using "I."

PREPARATION

- Select a well-written informational text (or set of texts for guided reading) on a topic of interest or curricular-related subject.

- Collect kid-friendly infographics to read closely, discuss, and analyze.

- Get enough clipboards and sticky notes for your whole class to record new learning in sketches or words.

EXPLANATION

When Stephanie Harvey spoke at the Illinois Reading Council Conference in March 2014, she said something about informational text that stuck with me—nonfiction is the most accessible genre for young children. Think about it. Nonfiction is accessible because children don't have to read every word to gain a lot of information. The images in informational texts have in-depth information. In fact, young readers often get more information from the images than they do from the text. This experience guides learners to carefully examine fact-packed visuals to glean information and assimilate new learning with their current background knowledge.

EXPERIENCE

Demonstration and Guided Practice

- Read a page or two of text or look at one aspect of the infographic. Show children how you draw or write about your new learning on a sticky note. Continue this process as you read the next few pages of the book or look at another aspect of the infographic.

- Invite readers or listeners to think and share with their partners about their new learning and draw or write about their new learning on a sticky note.

- Pose questions like these to nudge students' thinking:

  - What is the author trying to teach you?

  - Where in the text/image did you find that information? Let's "reread" the image to find out.

  - What proof does the author use?

  - How does what you've just learned fit with what you already know?

  - Do you have to revise your thinking?

  - Do you still have questions?

  - How can you go about finding the answers?

Release Responsibility

Make sticky notes available so that children can continue to record new learning while reading informational texts during guided or independent reading.

Transforming Literacy Teaching in the Era of Higher Standards, K–2 © 2015 by Maria P. Walther, Scholastic Teaching Resources

Big Idea: Integrate Illustrations, Images, and Text Features With Text

TRANSFORMING TEACHING	
The focus is more on the text and meaning of words and less on the interaction between text and illustrations.	The focus is balanced between the written words and building an awareness of the role illustrations and other graphic elements play in understanding the overall message.

Inquiry Experience: Use Illustrations to Describe Characters, Settings, and Events

TARGET

- I can look carefully at the illustrations in order to better understand the story.
- I can use illustrations to learn more about the characters' actions and feelings.
- I can study the illustrations to learn more about the setting.
- I can notice how the illustrations help me understand what is happening in the story.

PREPARATION

Select a wordless picture book (see chart below) or one that's nearly wordless in which the illustrations expand on the written message. (See chart on page 128.)

A Few of My Favorite Wordless Picture Books

Hank Finds an Egg (Dudley, 2013)	After several attempts to put the egg back in the nest, Hank perseveres and, with mother bird's help, figures out a way to return the egg right before it hatches.	
Journey (Becker, 2013)	This wordless picture book follows a girl on an imaginary journey. She uses her red crayon to draw her various modes of transportation.	
Mr. Wuffles (Wiesner, 2013)	Mr. Wuffles, the cat, doesn't play with any of his cat toys until one day he discovers a tiny alien spaceship. After Mr. Wuffles tosses it around, the insects help the aliens repair their ship and flee.	
Sea of Dreams (Nolan, 2011)	A young girl's carefully built sandcastle sits by the sea at dusk. Suddenly a light appears in the window, and a group of tiny travelers board a boat for an adventurous ride.	

A Few of My Favorite Nearly Wordless Picture Books

Ball (Sullivan, 2013)	Using only one word, *ball*, the illustrations in this book clearly depict the dog's feelings and dreams as he waits patiently for his ball-throwing companion to get home from school.
Bang (Timmers, 2011)	A book-reading deer is driving along and runs into a garbage can—"BANG"—causing a colorful chain-reaction.
Duck, Duck, Moose! (Bardhan-Quallen, 2014)	Two neat and tidy ducks prepare a surprise party for their clumsy roommate, Moose. Each time they make something, Moose unwittingly messes it up.
Stick! (Pritchett, 2013)	Puppy is excited to play with his new stick, but it takes a while to find someone who will play with him.

EXPLANATION

In addition to serving as ideal material for this learning experience, wordless and nearly wordless books enhance literacy knowledge in the following ways:

- Encourage language development
- Strengthen book handling concepts
- Develop a sense of story
- Offer opportunities for inferring

EXPERIENCE

Demonstration and Guided Practice

- To help students get in the habit of "reading the pictures," begin by showing them one striking image, like a photograph, art print, poster, or cartoon.
- Invite students to notice and tell the story of the image.
- Continue this part of the experience for a few days with different images.
- When you feel students are ready to think about a whole piece of connected text, introduce a wordless book. The first time read it straight through without stopping to converse. This gives children an overall sense of the story.
- At a later time, reread the text and illustrations, and notice and invite students to discuss how the illustrations achieve the following:
  - Move the plot forward
  - Give clues to upcoming actions and events
  - Develop the character(s)
  - Create a mood

Continue this experience throughout the year with other wordless and nearly wordless books.

Release Responsibility

- Offer opportunities for students to read wordless and nearly wordless books with a partner. Remind them to slow down and take the time to talk about each page.

- Place a basket of wordless books in the classroom for students to explore independently.

Inquiry Experience: Use Images and Text Features to Clarify Understanding

TARGET

I can look closely at and learn from images in informational texts.

PREPARATION

- Find a fact-filled image, like a photograph, diagram, map, graph, or infographic, that appears in a book on a page with minimal text.

- Create a T-Chart on a sheet of chart paper or in an electronic document; label the columns "New Learning" and "Still Wondering."

EXPLANATION

In this experience, along with teaching students how to carefully "read" the images found in informational texts, we are helping them build background for content-area learning, exposing them to academic vocabulary, and motivating them to seek more information about topics of interest.

EXPERIENCE

Demonstration and Guided Practice

- To help students get in the habit of doing "image research," begin by showing them one fact-filled image from a book, like a photograph, diagram, map, graph, or infographic without any text showing. (Cover up the text, if needed.)

- Ask students, "What can you learn by looking closely at this image?"

- Jot down their observations on the T-chart. Or you can have students record their own ideas on sticky notes and add them to the chart.

- Compare their image observations with the text from the book. Notice how much more information they learned from the visual image than they would have by simply reading the text.

- Over a number of days, continue this process with other visual images in the book to see what children can add to their new learning.

Release Responsibility

Remind students of this process when they are doing research for writing their own informational texts.

Big Idea: Compare and Contrast

TRANSFORMING TEACHING	
Familiar traditional tales are read aloud.	Familiar traditional tales are paired with less-familiar tales from various cultures.

Inquiry Experience: Share and Compare Traditional Tales

TARGETS

- I can notice how the adventures and experiences of characters are alike.
- I can notice how the adventures and experiences of characters are different.

PREPARATION

Collect traditional tales with similar motifs. See chart on page 131 for some suggested titles and guiding questions.

EXPLANATION

As you may have already noticed, many of your students lack a rich background in the traditional tales, including nursery rhymes. It is important that we bridge that gap for our students. These tales help readers make connections to future events. In fact, "experiences with this genre form an invaluable thread that connects past stories to other readings, music, or plays to be experienced in years to come" (Fuhler & Walther, 2007, p. 73). When students have opportunities to compare and contrast these tales, they deepen their understanding of story elements, text structures, and theme.

EXPERIENCE

Demonstration and Guided Practice

Share and compare traditional tales.

You might choose to begin an inquiry experience with traditional tales using the humorous picture book *The Princess and the Pig* (Emmett, 2011), which includes references to *Sleeping Beauty, Thumbelina, The Prince and the Pauper, Puss in Boots,* and *The Frog Prince.* Select two different versions of one of those tales to compare and contrast, focusing on the adventures and experiences of the characters.

Release Responsibility

- After your demonstration, divide your class into partnerships or small groups to share and compare other tales with similar motifs or different versions of the same tale from different cultures, like *Cinderella.* (See suggested tales and titles on page 131.)
- Invite students to record their findings in a way that makes sense to them.
- Provide time for students to share and compare their tales.

Comparing Tales With Similar Motifs

Motif	Tales	Questions
SUPERNATURAL VILLAINS	• *The Three Billy Goats Gruff* (Galdone, 1973/2001) • *Hansel and Gretel* (Marshall, 1990) • *Jack and the Beanstalk* (Kellogg, 1991)	Who is the villain in the story? How do the villain's actions impact the experiences and adventures of the other characters?
TRICKY ANIMALS	• *Red Riding Hood* (Marshall, 1987) • *The Three Little Pigs* (Marshall, 1989) • *Chicken Little* (Emberley, 2009) • *Prairie Chicken Little* (Hopkins, 2013)	Who is the trickster in the story? How do the trickster's actions impact the experiences and adventures of the other characters?
MAGICAL OBJECTS	• *Jack and the Beanstalk* (Kellogg, 1991) • *Strega Nona* (dePaola, 1975) • *The Talking Eggs* (San Souci, 1989) • *Two of Everything* (Hong, 1993)	What is the magical object in the story? How does the magical object impact the experiences and adventures of the other characters?
MAGICAL POWERS	• *The Magic Fish* (Littledale, 1966) • *The Seven Chinese Brothers* (Mahy, 1990)	Who has magical powers? How do their powers impact the experiences and adventures of the other characters?
MAGICAL TRANSFORMATION	• *Cinderella* (Marshall, 1989) • *The Gingerbread Boy* (Galdone, 1975) • *Señorita Gordita* (Ketteman, 2012)	Who makes a magical transformation? How does the transformation impact the experiences and adventures of the other characters?

COMPARING MULTICULTURAL VERSIONS OF A TRADITIONAL TALE

- Gather a multicultural text set. Here are a few of my favorite *Cinderella* versions:
  - *Adelita: A Mexican Cinderella Story* (dePaola, 2002)
  - *Mufaro's Beautiful Daughters* (Steptoe, 1987)
  - *Rough-Face Girl* (Martin, 1992)
  - *Yen-Shen: A Cinderella Story From China* (Louie, 1982)

- Collaborate with your class to create a set of questions to set a purpose for reading the different versions and frame their comparisons (Norton, 2003). Use these questions of the Cinderella story as a guide:
  - How is Cinderella related to the other characters in the story?
  - How does the author/illustrator show that Cinderella has a lowly position in the household?
  - Why is Cinderella going to miss the ball/special event?
  - How does she receive her wishes? Who helps her transform?

- Where does she meet the prince?
- How does she prove she's the real Cinderella?

- Create a chart similar to the one I made for the Cinderella stories, which is found in the online resources (see page 160), for students to chart their findings.

- Strategically pair or group students and let them select a version of the tale to read and chart, then share their findings with the class.

- Gather all of students' information on a master chart to display in your room or copy for future reference.

Cinderella Chart

Version	How Cinderella is related to other characters	Evidence of Cinderella's lowly position	Experience that causes her to miss ball/special event	How she receives her wishes/magical helper	Where she meets the prince	How she proves she's the real Cinderella	What happens to her other family members

Transforming Literacy Teaching in the Era of Higher Standards, K–2 © 2015 by Maria P. Walther, Scholastic Teaching Resources

Inquiry Experience: Compare and Contrast Two Informational Texts on the Same Topic

TARGETS

- I can compare and contrast how two informational texts on the same topic present their main ideas.
- I can compare and contrast how two informational texts on the same topic present key details.

Text 1 Title, Author	Text 2 Title, Author
Sun Up, Sun Down (Gibbons, 1983)	*The Sun Our Nearest Star* (Branley, 2002)
How a Seed Grows (Jordan, 1992)	*A Seed Is Sleepy* (Aston, 2007)
These Bees Count (Formento, 2012)	*Are You a Bee?* (Allen, 2004)

PREPARATION

Look for informational text pairs where the authors approach the topic in a different structure or style. For example, you might choose to have students compare a descriptive text to a question-answer text or a diagram to a paragraph.

Prepare a Venn diagram, H-Chart, or another graphic organizer to compare and contrast the two texts.

EXPLANATION

As students compare informational texts written in different formats, they will strengthen their ability to read carefully and notice techniques that they might incorporate in their own nonfiction pieces.

EXPERIENCE

Demonstration and Guided Practice

- Introduce the topic and the terms *similar* and *different* or *compare* and *contrast*.
- Read the first informational text. Jot down main idea, key details, and any other things students noticed about the text.
- The next day, read the second informational text and do the same.
- The third day, compare and contrast the two texts using the graphic organizer.

Release Responsibility

To release responsibility to learners, prompt and coach them as they compare and contrast texts during guided reading or conferences.

Transforming Literacy Teaching in the Era of Higher Standards, K–2 © 2015 by Maria P. Walther, Scholastic Teaching Resources

Chapter 7

Inquiry Experiences— Writing in Focus

The inquiry experiences in this chapter differ from those in Chapter 6 in that four of them (listed below) are designed to be teacher-guided writing units that take students through the writing-specific stages of the gradual release, including immersion, demonstration, and guided writing. These inquiry experiences may last a few weeks, so you probably won't repeat them over the course of the year.

Go online to view a video on Inquiry Experiences— Writing in Action; see page 160.

- Craft Pattern Books
- Pen a Personal Narrative
- Interview and Write a Biography
- Study and Write a "How-to" Piece

The other inquiry experiences are not as time consuming and can be repeated based on your learning context and students' needs. In the sample schedule on page 134, I've shown one way you might choose to organize these experiences across your year. The inquiry experiences are organized according to the "big idea" they address: Communicate Opinions, Convey Information, and Craft Narratives.

Quarter 1	Quarter 2	Quarter 3	Quarter 4
Craft Predictable and Pattern Books	Pen a Personal Narrative	Play With Words	Student Choice Writing
Share Opinions	Review a Book	Review a Book	Compare Books and Movies
Research and Write an Informational Text	Research and Write an Informational Text	Interview and Write a Biography	Study and Write a "How-to" Piece

Big Idea: Communicate Opinions

TRANSFORMING TEACHING	
Focus is primarily on narrative and expository writing.	Opinion-related conversations and writing opportunities occur throughout the year.

Inquiry Experience: Share Opinions

TARGETS

- I can state my opinion.
- I can give reasons for my opinion.
- I can write about my opinion.

PREPARATION

Think about places in your current curriculum where you can weave opinion-related conversations and writing into the learning experience. Gather a book or two that lead students to write about their opinions.

Books That Lead to Opinion-Sharing or Writing Experiences

The Greatest Dinosaur Ever (Guiberson, 2013)	In first-person point of view, each dinosaur argues why it was the greatest dinosaur of all. The books ends with the author asking, "So which dinosaur was the greatest?"
Lulu and the Brontosaurus (Viorst, 2010)	Bratty Lulu wants a brontosaurus for a pet, so she runs away to the forest to find one. The tables turn when the brontosaurus decides he wants Lulu for his pet. Viorst interjects her authorial voice throughout the book and offers readers three different ending options, leading to the question, "Which ending did you prefer and why?"

Sparky! (Offill, 2014)	A determined young girl convinces her mother to let her get a new pet sloth. After reading, invite children to discuss or write about whether they think a sloth would make a good pet.
What's Your Favorite Animal? (Carle, 2014)	"What is your favorite animal?" Eric Carle asked 14 different children's book artists this question and got 14 very different opinions. As you share this book with your students, discuss the various ways the artists went about answering the question. Notice the different styles and genres of writing. Then, ask your students the same question to discover their opinions.

EXPLANATION

Before we can expect students to write about their opinions, we have to provide them opportunities to orally share their opinions about a variety of topics. The most authentic opinion writing occurs when students have an opinion about a real-world event or want to share their opinion about a book or topic with others. So, in my opinion, the best teaching context for opinion writing is during reading workshop or content-area instruction.

EXPERIENCE

The learning experiences listed below are just a few opinion-sharing and writing opportunities to offer your young learners throughout the year:

- Capitalize on naturally occurring occasions for students to share their opinions and the reasons behind those opinions. Ask questions like, "What is your opinion of the [book, movie, classroom activity, field trip, website]?"

- Model writing your own opinions pieces or find age-appropriate opinion pieces to share. Look for editorials, petitions, persuasive letters, or speeches. You may need to modify the original text to make it more kid-friendly. Notice and name the characteristics of a well-crafted opinion piece.

- Chart the characteristics of strong opinion pieces to guide your students' writing. Here are some characteristics you might include:
  - Consider your audience.
  - Hook the reader.
  - State a BIG and BOLD opinion.
  - Provide reasons and examples.
  - Use connecting words.
  - Conclude in an interesting way.

- Provide opportunities for students to orally share or write mini-opinion pieces as responses to reading or other content-area studies.

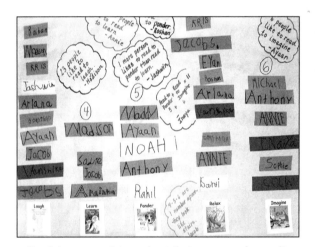

Graph learners opinions about their purposes for reading.

After studying owls, bats, and spiders, invite learners to state or write their opinions about these creatures and the reasons for their opinions.

Let's Write a Book Review!

Introduce the book to your readers—don't give away the ending!

Share what you liked (or didn't like) about the book. Explain your reasons.

Recommend this book (if you liked it) to your readers.
    What kind of reader would like this book? WHY?

Write shared book review guidelines.

Post book reviews on the bulletin board.

Inquiry Experience: Review a Book

TARGETS

- I can hook my reader.
- I can write about my opinion.
- I can give reasons for my opinion.
- I can recommend my book to a reader.

PREPARATION

- Collect examples of well-written book reviews to share with your students.
- For the first demonstration book review, select a book your students know well and love. For subsequent reviews, consider choosing a book your students did not enjoy.

EXPLANATION

I learned the importance of writing books reviews and the procedure outlined here from Regie Routman's book *Writing Essentials* (2005, p. 132). These are the reasons she gives for writing book reviews with your students. Book reviews:

- Develop writers' ability to write summaries.
- Help writers learn to make every word count.
- Encourage writers to choose words carefully so as to not give away surprises in, or the ending of, the book.
- Promote appreciation for books—post reviews on bulletin boards or share them with peers.

EXPERIENCE

Immersion in the Genre

- Immerse your students in well-written book reviews.
- Based on what you've learned from reading the examples, work with your students to write shared book review guidelines (Walther & Phillips, 2012, p. 149) like the ones my class created. (See picture above.)

Demonstration

- Demonstrate the process of writing a book review using the guidelines you created with your class. Note that the guidelines we created outline the three main parts of a book review, and each part is written in a different color. *I usually spend one mini-lesson on each section and write that section in the color that corresponds with the chart.*

- In a shared writing format, collaborate to write the introduction to your review.

- Introduce the connecting words and phrases shown in the box on page 137. Show how to use the selected words and phrases as you are writing multiple reasons for your shared opinion.

- Conclude the piece in an inventive way.

Guided Writing

After you feel you've modeled enough shared book reviews, release the responsibility to students to write their own book review. I usually have them proceed one section at a time, as I do in my demonstration.

Sharing and Celebrating

Invite students to create an illustration to go with the review and display the finished reviews on a bulletin board near the school library, for a family literacy night, or while the school is having a book fair.

Inquiry Experience: Compare Books and Movies

TARGETS

- I can state my opinion.
- I can give reasons for my opinion.
- I can write about my opinion.

PREPARATION

Select a book that has a short, animated movie version (not a full-length motion picture version) such as *The Snowman* (Briggs, 1978), *The Lorax* (Seuss, 1971), or books in the Arthur series by Marc Brown or the Magic School Bus Series by Joanna Cole. Many of the older, animated movie versions may be available at your public library.

EXPLANATION

This experience asks learners to gather and cite evidence from multiple and varied sources.

EXPERIENCE

Immersion

After reading and viewing, ask learners, "Which version did you prefer and why?"

Demonstration

- Begin in a shared writing format, writing an opinion piece using the characteristics of strong opinion pieces found on page 135.
- Draw students' attention to the visual images, changes in plot, the music in the movie, and their overall experience.

Guided Writing

Release responsibility by introducing another book-movie pair and inviting students to write their own opinion piece.

Sharing and Celebrating

Provide time for students to share and discuss their finished opinion pieces with partners, in small groups, or with the whole class.

Connecting Words and Phrases That Help Writers Explain More Than One Reason

- ❋ For example
- ❋ For instance
- ❋ Also
- ❋ In addition
- ❋ Furthermore
- ❋ Similarly
- ❋ Likewise
- ❋ Lastly
- ❋ Finally

Big Idea: Convey Information

TRANSFORMING TEACHING	
Procedural writing is taught as a separate genre.	Procedural writing is incorporated into the curriculum by demonstrating and providing opportunities for students to write about class procedures, science experiments, the results of inquiry learning experiences, and more.
Large research projects are conducted once or twice a year.	Students regularly engage in research and writing experiences that vary in depth and length of instructional time anywhere from two minutes to two weeks.
Students' informational pieces draw on nonfiction texts as a source.	Students write nonfiction pieces by gathering information from a variety of resources, including interviewing and primary source documents.

Inquiry Experience: Study and Write a "How-To" Piece

TARGET

I can use what I've learned from reading "how-to" texts to write my own how-to piece.

PREPARATION

Gather a collection of mentor texts and examples of procedural writing. If you have a guided-reading book room, don't forget to take a look in there. You may be surprised how many procedural texts are available at a variety of levels.

Procedural Writing Mentor Texts

How To (Morstad, 2013)	If you are looking for a book to spark ideas for procedural writing, this one fits the bill.
How to Teach a Slug to Read (Pearson, 2011)	In addition to being a mentor text for procedural writing, this would be the perfect book to read aloud to parents on curriculum night. It highlights the importance of reading aloud nursery rhymes, talking about vocabulary words, and repeated reading, all in a humorous way.
How to Wash a Woolly Mammoth (Robinson, 2013)	A young girl shares her step-by-step guide to bathing a pet woolly mammoth. This book would be an ideal mentor text for informational how-to pieces.

EXPLANATION

Informational text that gives directions or explains a process can be called instructional writing, procedural writing, or how-to writing. This sequentially organized writing is characterized by precise language. It is an engaging genre for young writers because it is purposeful writing about real-world topics.

EXPERIENCE

Immersion in the Genre

- Immerse students in the procedural writing genre by reading and discussing real-world examples like game or craft instructions, text excerpts like the "how-to" pages in the Scaredy Squirrel books by Melanie Watt, or the picture books listed on page 138.
- Create a shared definition of procedural writing.
- Notice and chart the characteristics of effective how-to pieces. (See the chart below.)

Demonstration

- Model creating your own procedural writing piece. Remember you can do these via the morning message throughout the year!

Guided Writing

- Invite students to write a how-to piece about a self-selected topic or something that aligns with your curriculum.

Sharing and Celebrating

- Use the shared definition and characteristics as a guide for self-assessment when students create their own procedural writing pieces.

A Few Procedural Writing Ideas to Get You Started	What Is Procedural (How-To) Writing?
• How to ask a friend to play • How to be an active listener • What to do during a fire drill/tornado drill • How to get to the nurse's office from our classroom • How to check out a library book • How to become a better reader • How we did our science experiment • How to solve a story problem • How to make a little book • How to write a story • How to dress for wintry weather • How to get ready to go home	• Begins by telling readers what they are going to make or do. • Lists the materials needed. • Uses connecting words and phrases like *first, next, then,* and *finally.* • Tells the order of how to do things, sometimes using numbered steps. • Starts instructions with an action word (verb). • Includes diagrams, labels, or illustrations to help readers.

Inquiry Experience: Research and Write an Informational Text

Create a text set.

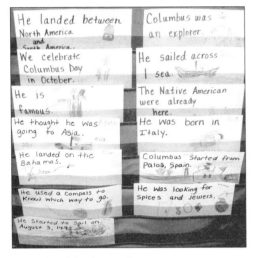

Record and display new learning.

TARGETS

- I can think like a researcher.
- I can work with my classmates to research and write about a topic.

PREPARATION

- Create a text set including informational texts, digital resources, songs, and/or poems about a famous person or content-area topic.
- Prepare paper (sentence strips or white paper cut to 4½- x 12-inches) or interactive whiteboard document for collecting brainstormed facts.
- Select a place to display gathered facts.

EXPLANATION

The purpose of this experience is to develop the skills and habits of mind of a researcher, including:

- Reading from multiple sources
- Restating and recording facts in their own words
- Determining an organizational structure for informational text
- Organizing the facts using the determined structure
- Revising to ensure information is clearly communicated

EXPERIENCE

DAY 1

1. Read and discuss a text or digital resource about the famous person or content-area topic.

2. Brainstorm and record nine to ten different facts from nine to ten different students. These facts will be used on Day 4 to make the class biography or informational text. Each child should have one fact by the end of the week. Remind each student to write his or her name on the fact. Instruct each child to draw a picture to accompany his or her fact. Display the facts.

DAY 2

1. Review facts collected on the previous day.

2. Read and discuss a new source.

   - Check the source's copyright date.
   - Notice how the text is organized.
   - Notice and discuss any similarities or differences between the two sources.

 Transforming Literacy Teaching in the Era of Higher Standards, K–2 © 2015 by Maria P. Walther, Scholastic Teaching Resources

3. Brainstorm and record nine to ten different facts from nine to ten different students and repeat the process outlined in Day 1. Record facts collected each day in a different color marker or font to delineate which facts came from which sources.

DAY 3—Continue with the same procedure as Day 1 & 2.

DAY 4—Organize the Class Biography or Informational Text.

1. Finish brainstorming facts for students who still do not have one; cut apart the chart (if needed) and give each student his or her fact.

2. Invite students to read their fact to a friend.

3. Discuss the events in the famous person's life or the structure that best communicate the information and divide facts into groups like beginning, middle, and end, or in categories like egg, larva, pupa, and adult. Assist students in finding their group.

4. Each group works together to arrange their facts in chronological order or in the order that matches their agreed-upon structure.

5. After each group agrees, place the whole biography or informational text in order. Read and revise, as needed.

Assist students as they work together to organize their facts.

Inquiry Experience: Interview Someone and Write a Biography

(Adapted from Month-by-Month Trait-Based Writing Instruction *[Walther & Phillips, 2009])*

TARGETS

- I can define a biography.
- I can explain how biographers find information about their subject.
- I can gather facts about a person.
- I can write an informational piece about that person.

PREPARATION

Gather engaging biographies to serve as mentor texts for the immersion portion of the genre exploration. Remember to read and discuss the author's notes that often include primary source documents and other helpful information. Some of my new favorites are found listed below.

A Few of My Favorite Biographies

| *Gandhi: A March to the Sea* (McGinty, 2013) | You can almost hear their footsteps in the rhythm of McGinty's words as you travel with Gandhi and his fellow protestors on their march to the sea. Create a text set with books about other peaceful protests like *We March* (Evans, 2012), *A Sweet Smell of Roses* (Johnson, 2007), *Freedom on the Menu: The Greensboro Sit-Ins* (Weatherford, 2007). |  |

I Am Abraham Lincoln (Meltzer, 2014)	This is one of the biographies in the "Ordinary People Change the World" series. These books are ideal for young readers because they are told in an engaging manner that connects with children, while also clearly illustrating the lasting importance of the accomplishments of each individual.
The Watcher: Jane Goodall's Life with the Chimps (Winter, 2011)	From the time she was a little girl, Jane was a "watcher" and always dreamed of living in Africa. Through determination, bravery, and hard work, this dream was fulfilled. Pair with *Me . . . Jane* (McDonnell, 2011).
Who Says Women Can't Be Doctors? The Story of Elizabeth Blackwell (Stone, 2013).	This inspiring biography about the first woman doctor is written in such a way that it will inform and entertain young readers at the same time. An author's note including a photograph of Blackwell adds to the information found in the book.

Select a subject for the biography. Depending on your grade level and students' writing ability, you might differentiate this selection in the following ways. In kindergarten, as a class, choose another staff member to write about, like the P. E. teacher, principal, or school librarian. In Grade 1, pair students with a classmate to be their "biography buddy" (Walther & Phillips, 2009). Grade 2 students could select a family or community member.

EXPLANATION

For Grades K–2, Writing Standard 8 states that students should be able to gather information from provided sources to answer a question. In addition, Speaking & Listening Standard 3 states that students should be able to ask and answer questions about what a speaker says. By incorporating interviewing and primary source documents into the writing process, this budding biographer exploration broadens students' experiences as informational writers.

EXPERIENCE

Immersion in the Genre

As you read and discuss the mentor texts, ask students to identify characteristics that are specific to this genre and chart the findings. In addition, you can encourage students to notice specific craft elements that make each biography interesting and unique.

Prewriting

- Discuss the role of interviewing and collecting primary source documents.

- Collaborate with your students to brainstorm possible interview questions. (See possible staff member questions on page 143.)

- Support students as they create their own interview questions and think about what kind of primary source documents they might request from their subject.

What Is a Biography?

* A nonfiction book about a person. (Lizzy)
* Written using "he" or "she." (pronouns)
* Describes the person's life, actions and relationships.
* Includes interesting details & lesser-known facts.

How do biographers research?

* Read books. (Sami) Go to library. (Xara)
* Watch the history channel. (Anthony)   * Ask someone about the person. (Anne)
* Search on the computer.   INTERVIEW! (Ryan)

What we noticed...

* Some are full/complete—from birth to death. (Samantha)
* Some are partial. (Sami)
* Biographies teach us what is was like back then. (Kendall)
* Biographies teach people about other people. (Sam)
* They teach us facts about someone real. (Aidan)

Chart students' findings as you read and discuss biographies.

Transforming Literacy Teaching in the Era of Higher Standards, K–2 © 2015 by Maria P. Walther, Scholastic Teaching Resources

- Once questions are written, guide students to categorize questions to help organize their information. Below are some suggestions.

Possible Staff Member Categories	Possible Buddy Categories	Possible Family/Community Member Categories
HOME • Where do you live? • Who is in your family?	Family	Background/Education
SCHOOL • Where did you go to school? • What was your favorite subject?	Favorites	Memories/Accomplishments
HOBBIES • What do you like to do when you're not at school?	Fun Facts	Hobbies/Interests
	Future	Life Lessons Learned

Interviewing and Gathering Primary Source Documents

- Explain that children will be interviewing their biography subject about their first category today.
- Model interviewing one of your students while the rest of the class observes, fishbowl style (you and the student in the middle of the circle, the rest of the class sitting in a circle observing).
- Provide time for students to conduct their interviews.
- When finished with the interviews, invite each student to share one interesting tidbit they learned about the staff member, buddy, or family/community member.

Writing a Biography Beginning

- Go back to the biography mentor texts that you read to the class and jot down the beginning lines of each book on a sticky note, interactive whiteboard document, or chart like the one pictured on page 144.

Discuss what students notice about the different types of beginnings in the biographies you read together. Give examples of how different students might use one of the leads in their own biography. (Again, see chart, page 144.) Then, choose your own lead and demonstrate writing the introduction to your biography.

- Provide time for students to craft their biography beginning.
- Next, demonstrate how a writer takes the information from his or her interview and organizes it into meaningful sentences about the person.

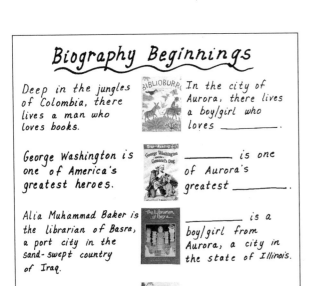

Biography Beginnings

Deep in the jungles of Colombia, there lives a man who loves books.

In the city of Aurora, there lives a boy/girl who loves _____.

George Washington is one of America's greatest heroes.

_____ is one of Aurora's greatest _____.

Alia Muhammad Baker is the librarian of Basra, a port city in the sand-swept country of Iraq.

_____ is a boy/girl from Aurora, a city in the state of Illinois.

In the wilds of Kentucky, 1809, a boy was born.

In the city of Aurora, 2011, a boy/girl lived.

Jot down the beginning lines of the biographies you've read.

- Provide time for students to write the first page of their biography.

- Before moving on to the second category, show students how you go about revising and editing your first page. Invite students to do the same.

Completing the Biography

Students continue interviewing, writing, revising, and editing until the biography is complete.

Polish and Present

Once students have completed the interview and writing process, provide them an opportunity to make a fancy cover for their biography. Begin by brainstorming possible titles. Then, invite students to write their title and illustrate their cover. You might consider teaching children how to write an author's note to wrap up their biography.

Big Idea: Craft Narratives

TRANSFORMING TEACHING	
Students write journal entries and stories.	Students regularly engage in narrative writing experiences that vary in depth and length.

Inquiry Experience: Craft Pattern Books

TARGET

I can use what I've learned from reading pattern mentor texts to write my own book.

PREPARATION

- Gather a variety of predictable and pattern mentor texts—both fiction and informational—with structures like list books, question and answer, days of the week, see-saw structure, cumulative (add-on) stories, and circular stories. See the list on page 146 for some suggested titles.

- Prepare blank little books for students. See pages 65–66 for an explanation.

EXPLANATION

We've long known the value of predictable and pattern books for beginning readers. The following supportive structures are also helpful scaffolds for beginning writers:

- Predictable plots

- Familiar sequences, like days of the week and counting

- Repetitive words and phrases
- Repetitive language patterns

In this experience, I use predictable and pattern books as a jumping-off point when children begin writing in their little books. If students choose to write other types of texts, like stories, informational texts, "how-to" books, and so on, I celebrate and encourage them to continue.

EXPERIENCE

Immersion in the Genre

While closely studying predictable and pattern books, discuss these questions:

- What do you notice about the book? Is the book fiction or nonfiction/informational?
- What decisions did the author make as a writer?
- What decisions did the illustrator make?
- Why do you think they made those decisions?
- Where do you think they got their ideas?
- What decisions will you make in your writing?

Immerse students in books with different structures.

PREWRITING

Invite students to brainstorm possible topics for their little book. Have them choose one from their list.

DEMONSTRATION AND GUIDED WRITING

Demonstrate crafting your own little book and/or create shared books as a class using what you've learned from the patterns you've studied. I often combine patterns to show children the possibilities. Invite students to do the same.

Sharing and Celebrating

During whole-class share, connect students' writing to the mentor text you've shared by asking some of the questions that appear above.

Once students have completed a few little books using what they've learned from the immersion process, invite them to reflect on and formatively assess their work. One way to do this is by having them fill out the form found in the online resources (see page 160), *Reading Like a Writer: Thinking About My Little Books*, which asks students what they notice in their own writing, what they think is their best piece of writing thus far, ideas for future writing, and goals for future writing.

Inquiry Experience: Pen a Personal Narrative

(Adapted from: Month-by-Month Trait-Based Writing Instruction *[Walther & Phillips, 2009] and* Month-by-Month Reading Instruction for the Differentiated Classroom *[Walther & Phillips, 2012])*

TARGETS

- I can define a personal narrative.
- I can write a personal narrative about a memorable event.

BOOKS WITH A LIST PATTERN

- *Beetle Bop* (Fleming, 2007)
- *Chicken Cheeks* (Black, 2009)
- *Lots of Dots* (Frazier, 2010)
- *Move!* (Jenkins & Page, 2006) (Informational)
- *Things I Like* (Browne, 1989)

BOOKS WITH A QUESTION-ANSWER PATTERN

- *Does a Kangaroo Have a Mother, Too?* (Carle, 2000)
- *What Do You Do With a Tail Like This?* (Jenkins & Page, 2003) (Informational)
- *Where Is the Green Sheep?* (Fox, 2004)
- *Yes Day!* (Rosenthal, 2009)

BOOKS WITH A DAYS-OF-THE-WEEK PATTERN

- *Always in Trouble* (Demas, 2009)
- *Dog Days of School* (DiPucchio, 2014)
- *Perfect Square* (Hall, 2011)
- *Pigs to the Rescue* (Himmelman, 2010)

BOOKS WITH A SEE-SAW PATTERN

- *First the Egg* (Seeger, 2007) (Informational)
- *Fortunately* (Charlip, 1964)
- *Good News Bad News* (Mack, 2012)
- *Tough Boris* (Fox, 1994)

CUMULATIVE OR "ADD-ON" STORIES

- *The Book That Zack Wrote* (Long, 2011)
- *My Friend Rabbit* (Rohmann, 2002)
- *There Was an Old Monster!* (Emberley, Emberley, & Emberley, 2009)

CIRCULAR STORIES

- *When a Monster Is Born* (Taylor, 2006)

PREPARATION

Gather engaging picture books written in first-person point of view to serve as mentor texts for the immersion portion of the inquiry experience. Some of my favorites are listed below.

A Few of My Favorite Texts Written in First-Person Point of View

Picture Day Perfection (Diesen, 2013)	A boy has planned all year for the "perfect" picture and all of his hard work is ruined when he smiles.	
Recess at 20 Below (Aillaud, 2005)	Experience recess in Alaska, told from a young student's perspective.	
Saturdays and Teacakes (Laminack, 2004)	Every Saturday a young boy pedals his bicycle to visit his Grandmother. Set in rural Alabama in 1964, Soentpiet's detailed watercolor illustrations capture the mood of this beautifully crafted descriptive memoir.	

EXPLANATION

This genre exploration focuses on the close study and crafting of a personal narrative text. The purpose of this experience is to lead students to discover specific characteristics of the genre, create a shared list of criteria about what makes an effective personal narrative, and then invite children to apply their understandings to craft their own personal story.

EXPERIENCE

Immersion in the Genre

As you read and discuss the mentor texts, ask students to identify characteristics that are specific to this genre and chart the findings. In addition, you can encourage students to notice specific craft elements that make the personal narrative genre interesting and unique.

Prewriting

- Model creating your own planning sheet for the personal narrative that you will be writing along with the students.

- Orally rehearse your piece. Invite students to ask you questions about the event you've chosen, so you can demonstrate how answering their specific questions helps you add details to your story.

- Divide students into pairs or groups of three and provide time for them to orally rehearse their pieces.

Writing a Personal Narrative Lead and Introduction

Go back to the personal narrative mentor texts that you read to the class and jot down the beginning lines of each book on a sticky note, chart, or interactive whiteboard document like the one pictured below.

Sample Personal Narrative Leads

Fancy Nancy: Bonjour, Butterfly (O'Connor, 2008)	Don't you think butterflies are exquisite?
Ira Sleeps Over (Waber, 1972/2000)	I was invited to sleep at Reggie's house.
Saturdays and Teacakes (Laminack, 2004)	When I was nine or ten years old, I couldn't wait for Saturdays.
Sloppy Joe (Keane, 2009)	Mom says I'm the first kid in history to . . .

Discuss what students notice about the different types of leads in the personal narratives you read together. Give examples of how different students might use one of the leads in their own personal narratives. Then, choose your own lead and model writing the introduction to your personal narrative. Remind students that the introduction should tell readers what the narrative is going to be about.

Moving Your Story Through Time With Connecting Words or Phrases

Reread, revise, and edit the page that you wrote the day before. Then, continue writing by discussing the use of connecting words and phrases. Choose an appropriate word or phrase for the next page of your personal narrative. Write aloud to help students hear you think through your choices as a writer.

Rereading, Revising, and Drafting

Continue to demonstrate how writers reread, revise, and edit each time they begin to write again. Model writing page 3 of your narrative. Guide and confer with students as they write their page. Continue in the same fashion for page 4.

Crafting the Big Ending

- Create an anchor chart with different types of endings that students could use to end their pieces.

Chart the characteristics of personal narratives.

Moving Your Story Through Time With Connecting Words or Phrases		The Big Ending	
First In the morning	Next In the afternoon	*I will never forget . . .* (The thing you remember the most about the experience)	*I learned that . . .* (Something that you learned from the experience)
Later After	Finally In the end After such a busy day	*I was _____ when . . .* (How you felt about the experience)	*The best thing about _____ was . . .*

Share and celebrate writers' personal narratives.

- Share the different types of endings on the chart. Discuss with students which ending would make the most sense for their personal narrative. Provide time for students to think and share with their partners. Model selecting the best ending for your narrative, and then write the ending down.

Polish and Present: Creating a Title and "Fancy" Cover

Display the covers of the personal narratives you read during the immersion experience. Notice the characteristics of a picture book cover including, but not limited to, the following:

- The title is near the top and written in big letters.

- The author's name appears on the cover.

- A detailed, colorful illustration shows something important that happens in the narrative.

Big Idea: Create Poetry

TRANSFORMING TEACHING	
Poetry writing mainly occurs during poetry month in April and often focuses on various poetic forms, like acrostic poems and haiku.	Poetry writing is incorporated throughout the year, and children are encouraged to write free-form poems about topics of interest or as a reading response.

Inquiry Experience: Play With Words

TARGET

I can use what I've learned from listening to and reading poetry to write my own poems.

PREPARATION

- Gather a variety of poetry books for immersion.
- Prepare 3- x 8-inch strips for use in the pocket chart or on an interactive whiteboard document to record nouns, verbs, and adjectives.
- Strategically pair learners with a poetry pal.
- Prepare a small zippered plastic bag with about 25 1½- x 5-inch paper strips for each pair.

A Sampling of Poetry Mentor Texts

Face Bug (Lewis, 2013)	Welcome to the Face Bug Museum with close-up photographs and poems about 14 different bugs. Ends with "And Now a Word from Our Bugs," which tells readers, in first-person point of view, where each bug lives, how it grows, what it eats, and what eats it.
Follow, Follow (Singer, 2013)	In Singer's sequel to the book *Mirror, Mirror,* she creates another collection of "reverso" poems about fairy tales. These are ideal poems for showing how poets play with words!
Hi, Koo! A Year of Seasons (Muth, 2014)	Join Koo the panda bear on a joyful journey through the seasons while reading this beautifully illustrated collection of 26 poems. It is important to read the author's note before sharing this book with your students, as Muth has chosen not to adhere to the rigid structure of the five-seven-five syllable pattern for haiku.
Seeds, Bees, Butterflies, and More! Poems for Two Voices (Gerber, 2013)	Pair your students for some poetry reading fun! Together, they can read Gerber's rhyming poems and learn about nature. This book is ideal for plant units and for sharing in the spring.

EXPLANATION

Although the standards for narrative writing don't specifically call for poetry writing, I believe it is essential for students to write poetry in order to better analyze the craft and structure of poetry. This belief is echoed by poet, educator, and writer Sara Holbrook, who shared the following reasons to read and write poetry with students (Judson's Literacy in Motion Conference, 2014). Poetry:

- Helps children make connections through shared experiences

- Engages students because they like poetry and it's fun to read and write

- Serves as vehicle for literacy and learning across all content areas

- Creates authentic teaching opportunities because every poem is a mini-lesson

- Provides children with a chance to write about events that have touched their hearts

- Encourages writers to practice being precise and concise

This learning experience can be repeated throughout the year. Start early in the year by creating shared poems. Later, release the responsibility to students, showing them how to use poetry as a way to summarize new learning about a science or social studies topic, respond to a text, or record a shared experience such as a field trip.

Strategically pair learners with a poetry pal.

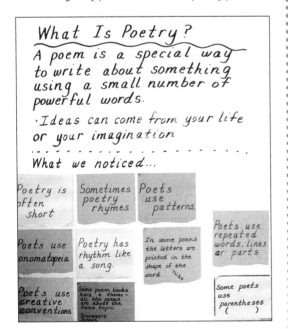

Notice and chart the characteristics of engaging poems.

EXPERIENCE

Immersion in the Genre

- Immerse students in the genre of poetry by reading and discussing a variety of poems.

- Create a shared definition of poetry.

- Notice and chart the characteristics of engaging poems. (See anchor chart at left.)

Prewriting

- Select a specific topic that you and your students have studied.

- Invite learners to share nouns, verbs, or adjectives about that topic, and record each response on a separate 3- x 8-inch strip for use in the pocket chart or on an interactive whiteboard document.

- Collaborate with your learners to move the words around and add other words, as needed, to create a poem.

- Mix up the words and repeat the process, highlighting how a poet is constantly revising or playing with words.

- Continue with this demonstration until you feel that students are ready to try it on their own.

Poetry Pals Playing With Words

Strategically pair learners with a poetry pal. Give each pair a small zippered bag with about 25 1½- x 5-inch paper strips. Invite children to record a noun, verb, or adjective about a topic of their choice on each strip. Then, as you demonstrated to the whole class, have pairs play with the words until they've made a poem, adding additional words as needed.

Polish and Present

- Once students have had ample time to play with their poetry strips, give students poetry paper (see the online resources, page 160) to record their favorite poems and create accompanying illustrations.

- After students write their own poems, use the shared definition and characteristics as a guide for self-assessment.

- Provide opportunities for students to share their poems with their peers, cross-age buddies, or by recording a podcast to view at a later time.

(Adapted from Month-by-Month Reading Instruction for the Differentiated Classroom *[Walther & Phillips, 2012])*

Looking Back, Moving Forward

Your professional judgment is key when selecting from this menu of inquiry experiences and integrating them into your days, weeks, and months. One of the best ways to make these decisions is with a wise colleague or two at your side. The professional conversations you have will help deepen your understanding of the standards and the reflections you share after trying out an experience will strengthen your practice. To guide you in your planning, the online resources (see page 160) include tools that you may find helpful in organizing your instruction.

Professional Resources Cited

Allen, P. A. (2009). *Conferring: The keystone of a reader's workshop.* Portland, ME: Stenhouse.

Allington, R. L. (2006). *What really matters for struggling readers: Designing research-based programs* (2nd ed.). Boston: Allyn & Bacon.

Allington, R. L. (2013). What really matters when working with struggling readers. *The Reading Teacher, 66*(7), 520–530.

Anderson, J. (2005). *Mechanically inclined: Building grammar, usage, and style into writer's workshop.* Portland, ME: Stenhouse.

Anderson, J. (2007). Unconventional conventions: Teaching grammar and mechanics. *Adolescent Literacy In Perspective*, May/June, 2–4.

Anderson, J. (2014). What writing is and isn't. *Educational Leadership, 71*(7), 10–14.

Atwell, N. (2007). *The Reading Zone.* New York: Scholastic.

Beck, I. L., McKeown, M. G., & Kucan, L. (2013). *Bringing words to life: Robust vocabulary instruction* (2nd ed). New York: Guilford.

Bennett, S. (2007). *That workshop book: New systems and structures for classrooms that read, write, and think.* Portsmouth, NH: Heinemann.

Biggs-Tucker, K., & Tucker, B. (2015). *Transforming literacy teaching in the era of higher standards.* New York: Scholastic.

Blachowicz, C. L., & Fisher, P. (2000). Vocabulary instruction. In M. L. Kamil, P. B. Mosenthal, P. D. Pearson, & R. Barr (Eds.). *Handbook of reading research* (Vol. 3, pp. 503–523). Mahwah, NJ: Lawrence Erlbaum.

Blachowicz, C., & Ogle, D. (2001). *Reading comprehension: Strategies for independent learners.* New York: Guilford.

Boushey, G., & Moser, J. (2014). *The daily 5: Fostering literacy independence in the elementary grades* (2nd ed.). Portland, ME: Stenhouse.

Calkins, L., Ehrenworth, M., & Lehman, C. (2012). *Pathways to the common core: Accelerating achievement.* Portsmouth, NH: Heinemann.

Chappuis, J. (2009). *Seven strategies of assessment for learning.* Boston: Pearson.

Charlesworth, L. (2009). *Introduction to nonfiction: Write-on/wipe-off flip chart.* New York: Scholastic.

Clay, M. M. (2000). *Concepts about print: What have children learned about the way we print language?* Portsmouth, NH: Heinemann.

Cunningham, P. M. (2009). *Phonics they use: Words for reading and writing* (5th ed.). Boston: Allyn & Bacon.

Cunningham, P. M. (2009). *What really matters in vocabulary: Research-based practices across the curriculum.* Boston: Allyn & Bacon.

Duke, N. (2000). 3.6 minutes a day: The scarcity of informational texts in first grade. *Reading Research Quarterly*, 35, 202–224.

Fisher, D., & Frey, N. (2012). Close reading in elementary schools. *The Reading Teacher, 66*(3), 179–188.

Fountas, I. C., & Pinnell, G. S. (1999). *Matching books to readers: Using leveled books in guided reading K–3.* Portsmouth, NH: Heinemann.

Fountas, I. C., & Pinnell, G. S. (2009). *The Fountas & Pinnell leveled book list, K–8+: 2010–2012 edition.* Portsmouth, NH: Heinemann.

Fuhler, C. J., & Walther, M. P. (2007). *Literature is back!: Using the best books for teaching readers and writers across genres.* New York: Scholastic.

Harvey, S., & Daniels, H. (2009). *Comprehension & collaboration: Inquiry circles in action.* Portsmouth, NH: Heinemann.

Hiebert, E. H. (2012). *7 actions that teachers can take right now: Text complexity.* Retrieved from textproject.org/professional-development/text-matters/7-actions-that-teachers-can-take-right-now-text-complexity/

Hoyt, L. (2002). *Make it real: Strategies for success with informational texts.* Portsmouth, NH: Heinemann.

International Reading Association. (2000). *Excellent reading teachers: A position statement of the International Reading Association.* Newark, DE: Author.

International Reading Association Common Core State Standards (CCSS) Committee. (2012). *Literacy implementation guidance for the ELA Common Core State Standards* [White paper]. Retrieved from http://www.reading.org/Libraries/association-documents/ira_ccss_guidelines.pdf

Johnston, P. H. (2012). *Opening minds: Using language to change lives.* Portland, ME: Stenhouse.

Johnston, P. H. (2004). *Choice words: How our language affects children's learning.* Portland, ME: Stenhouse.

Keene, E. O. (2012). *Talk about understanding: Rethinking classroom talk to enhance comprehension.* Portsmouth, NH: Heinemann.

Keene, E. O., & Zimmerman, S. (2013). Years later, comprehension strategies still at work. *The Reading Teacher, 66*(8), 601–606.

Kiefer, B., Hepler, W., & Hickman, J. (2007). *Charlotte Huck's children's literature* (6th ed.). Boston: McGraw-Hill.

Laminack, L. L., & Wadsworth, R. M. (2012). *Bullying hurts: Teaching kindness through read alouds and guided conversations.* Portsmouth, NH: Heinemann.

Macon, J. M., Bewell, D., & Vogt, M. (1991). *Responses to literature.* Newark, DE: IRA.

McGill-Franzen, A., Allington, R. L., Yokoi, L, & Brooks, G. (1999). Putting books in the room seems necessary but not sufficient. *Journal of Educational Research, 93*, 67–74.

Miller, D. (2013a). I can create mental images to retell and infer big ideas. *The Reading Teacher, 66*(5), 360–364.

Miller, D. (2013b). *Reading with meaning: Teaching comprehension in the primary grades* (2nd ed.). Portland, ME: Stenhouse.

Miller, D., & Kelley, S. (2014). *Reading in the wild: The book whisperer's keys to cultivating lifelong reading habits.* San Francisco: Jossey-Bass.

Miller, D., & Moss, B. (2013). *No more independent reading without support.* Portsmouth, NH: Heinemann.

Nagy, W. E., & Townsend, D. (2012). Words as tools: Learning academic vocabulary as language acquisition. *Reading Research Quarterly, 47*(1), 91–108.

National Association for the Education of Young Children (NAEYC) and the Fred Rogers Center for Early Learning and Children's Media. (2012). *Technology and interactive media as tools in early childhood programs serving children from birth through age 8.* Washington, DC: Authors.

National Commission on Writing. (2003, April). *The neglected r: The need for a writing revolution.*

National Governors Association Center for Best Practices (NGA Center) and Council of Chief State School Officers (CCSSO) (2010). *Common core state standards initiative.* Washington, D.C.: Authors.

NGSS Lead States. (2013). *Next generation science standards: For states, by states.* Washington, DC: The National Academies Press.

Northwest Regional Educational Laboratory. (1999). *Seeing with new eyes: A guidebook on teaching and assessing beginning writers using the six-trait writing model* (5th ed.). Portland, OR: Author.

Norton, D. E. (2003). *Through the eyes of a child: An introduction to children's literature.* (6th ed.). Upper Saddle River, NJ: Merrill.

Opitz, M. F., Ford, M. P, & Erekson, J. A. (2011). *Accessible assessment: How 9 sensible techniques can power data-driven reading instruction*. Portsmouth, NH: Heinemann.

Pearson, P. D., & Gallagher, M. C. (1983). The instruction of reading comprehension. *Contemporary Educational Psychology, 8*, 317–344.

Pressley, M., Dolezal, S. E., Raphael, L. M., Mohan, L, Roehrig, A. D., & Bogner, K. (2003). *Motivating primary-grade students*. New York: Guilford.

Raphael, T. W. (1986). Teaching question answer relationships, revisited. *The Reading Teacher, 39*(6), 515–522.

Ray, K. W., & Cleaveland, L. B. (2004). *About the authors: Writing workshop with our youngest writers*. Portsmouth, NH: Heinemann.

Ray, K. W. & Laminack, L. L. (2001). *The writing workshop: Working through the hard parts (and they're all hard parts)*. Urbana, IL: NCTE.

Richardson, J. (2009). *The next step in guided reading: Focused assessment and targeted lessons for helping every student become a better reader*. New York: Scholastic.

Richardson, J., & Walther, M. (2013). *The next step guided reading assessment K–2*. New York: Scholastic.

Reutzel, D. R., Jones, C. D., & Newman, T. H. (2010). Scaffolded silent reading: Improving the conditions of silent reading practice. In Heibert, E. H., & Reutzel, D. R. (Eds.). *Revisiting silent reading: New directions for teachers and researchers*. (pp. 129–150). Newark, DE: International Reading Association.

Roskos, K., & Neuman, S. B. (2012). Formative assessment: Simply, no additives. *The Reading Teacher 65*(8), 534–538.

Routman, R. (2004). *Writing essentials: Raising expectations and results while simplifying teaching*. Portsmouth, NH: Heinemann.

Routman, R. (2008). *Teaching essentials: Expecting the most and getting the best from every learner, K–8*. Portsmouth, NH: Heinemann.

Scanlon, D. M., & Vellutino, F. R. (1997). A comparison of the instructional backgrounds and cognitive profiles of poor, average, and good readers who were initially identified as at risk for reading failure. *Scientific Studies of Reading, 1*, 191–216.

Smith, M. W., & Wilhelm, J. (2006). What research tells us about teaching grammar. *Voices from the Middle, 13*(4), 40–43.

Stuhlman, M. W., & Pianta, R. C. (2009). Profiles of educational quality in first grade. *The Elementary School Journal, 109*(4), 323–342.

Spandel, V. (2007). *Creating young writers*. Boston: Allyn & Bacon.

Taberski, S. (2011). *Comprehension from the ground up: Simplified, sensible instruction for the K–3 reading workshop*. Portsmouth, NH: Heinemann.

Walther, M. P., & Fuhler, C. J. (2010). *Teaching struggling readers with poetry*. New York: Scholastic.

Walther, M. P., & Phillips, K. A. (2009), *Month-by-month trait-based writing instruction*. New York: Scholastic.

Walther, M. P., & Phillips, K. A. (2012). *Month-by-month reading instruction for the differentiated classroom*. New York: Scholastic.

Wiggins, G., & McTighe, J. (2011). *The understanding by design guide to creating high-quality units*. Alexandria, VA: ASCD.

Yopp, H. K. (1992). Developing phonemic awareness in young children. *The Reading Teacher, 45*, 696–703.

Children's Literature Cited

CHAPTER 1: PLANTING THE SEEDS

Bishop, N. (2010). *Lizards.* New York: Scholastic.

Branley, F. (1986/2000). *Snow is falling.* New York: HarperCollins.

Breen, S. (2013). *Pug & Doug.* New York: Dial.

Carle, E. (1969/1987). *The very hungry caterpillar.* New York: Philomel.

Freedman, D. (2013). *The story of Fish and Snail.* New York: Viking.

Pattou, E. (2001). *Mrs. Spitzer's garden.* New York: Harcourt.

Pinkwater, D. M. (1977). *The big orange splot.* New York: Scholastic.

Seeger, L. V. (2013). *Bully.* New York: Roaring Brook.

Woodson, J. (2012). *Each kindness.* New York: Penguin.

CHAPTER 2: DISCOVERING CONNECTIONS

Bloom, B. (1999). *Wolf!* New York: Orchard.

Bromley, N. (2013). *Open very carefully: A book with bite.* Somerville, MA: Candlewick.

Buehner, C. (2001). *Superdog: The heart of a hero.* New York: HarperCollins.

Cabatingan, E. (2013). *Musk Ox counts.* New York: Roaring Brook.

Czekaj, J. (2011). *Cat secrets.* New York: HarperCollins.

Fleming, C. (2010). *Clever Jack takes the cake.* New York: Schwartz & Wade.

Hamm, M. (2004). *Winners never quit.* New York: HarperCollins.

Lichtenheld, T. (2011). *Cloudette.* New York: Holt.

Long, E. (2013). *The Wing Wing Brothers carnival de math.* New York: Holiday House.

McKinlay, M. (2011). *No bears.* Somerville, MA: Candlewick.

Piper, W. (1930). *The little engine that could.* New York: Platt & Munk.

Reynolds, P. (2003). *The dot.* Cambridge, MA: Candlewick.

Schaefer, L. M. (2013). *Lifetime: The amazing numbers in animal lives.* San Francisco: Chronicle.

Willems, M. (2007). *Today I will fly!* New York: Hyperion.

Willems, M. (2010). *We are in a book!* New York: Hyperion.

Yates, L. (2013). *Dog loves counting.* New York: Knopf.

CHAPTER 3: ELEVATING READING WORKSHOP

Arnold, T. (2013). *Fly Guy presents: Sharks.* New York: Scholastic.

Aston, D. H. (2007). *A seed is sleepy.* San Francisco: Chronicle.

Berger, B. (1984). *Grandfather Twilight.* New York: Putnam.

Bishop, N. (2010). *Lizards.* New York: Scholastic.

Brinckloe, J. (1985). *Fireflies.* New York: Simon & Schuster.

Bunting, E. (1988). *How many days to America?* Boston: Houghton Mifflin.

Cooke, L. (2013). *A little book of sloth.* New York: Simon & Schuster.

Davies, N. (2005). *Surprising sharks.* Cambridge, MA: Candlewick.

Denver, J. (2005). *Take me home, country roads.* Nevada City, CA: Dawn.

Donaldson, J. (2012). *Superworm.* New York: Scholastic.

Emberley, R., Emberley, A., & Emberley, E. (2009). *There was an old monster!* New York: Orchard.

Himmelman, J. (1998). *A dandelion's life.* New York: Children's Press.

Joyce, W. (2012). *The fantastic flying books of Mr. Morris Lessmore*. New York: Atheneum.

Judge, L. (2013). *How big were dinosaurs?* New York: Roaring Brook.

Klausmeier, J. (2013). *Open this little book*. San Francisco, CA: Chronicle.

Littledale, F. (1966). *The magic fish*. New York: Scholastic.

Llewellyn, C. (2000). *Earthworms*. New York: Scholastic.

Offill, J. (2014). *Sparky!* New York: Schwartz & Wade.

Pearson, T. C. (2013). *Elephant's story*. New York: Farrar Straus.

Piehl, J. (2011). *Let's look at sloths*. Minneapolis, MN: Lerner.

Prelutsky, J. (1983). *The Random House book of poetry for children*. New York: Random House.

Prelutsky, J. (1990). *Something big has been here*. New York: Greenwillow.

Prelutsky, J. (2008). *My dog may be a genius*. New York: Greenwillow.

Raposo, J., & Lichtenheld, T. (2013). *Sing*. New York: Henry Holt.

Roemer, H. B. (2004). *Come to my party and other shape poems*. New York: Holt.

Sayre, A. P. (2013). *Eat like a bear*. New York: Holt.

Sheehan, K. (2014). *The dandelion's tale*. New York: Schwartz & Wade.

Soto, G. (1993). *Too many tamales*. New York: Putnam.

Staake, B. (2014). *My pet book*. New York: Random House.

Starr, R. (2014). *Octopus's garden*. New York: Simon & Schuster.

Vicker, L. (2006). *Poetry parade*. Ames, IA: Unpublished personal teaching materials.

Weatherford, C. B. (2005). *Freedom on the menu: The Greensboro sit-ins*. New York: Dial.

Weiss, E. (2008). *From seed to dandelion*. New York: Scholastic.

Wheeler, E. (2013). *Miss Maple's seeds*. New York: Penguin.

CHAPTER 4: ENHANCING WRITING WORKSHOP

Fleming, C. (2012). *Oh, no!* New York: Schwartz & Wade.

Hanlon, A. (2012). *Ralph tells a story*. Las Vegas, NV: Amazon.

Hills, T. (2012). *Rocket writes a story*. New York: Schwartz & Wade.

Hills, T. (2010). *How Rocket learned to read*. New York: Schwartz & Wade.

Hood, S. (2014). *Rooting for you: A moving up story*. New York: Hyperion.

Hoppe. (2011). *The woods*. San Francisco: Chronicle.

Johnston, T. (2014). *Winter is coming*. New York: Simon & Schuster.

Kirk. (2007). *The library mouse*. New York: Abrams.

LaRochelle, D. (2012). *It's a tiger!* San Francisco: Chronicle.

Mack, J. (2012). *Frog and Fly: Six slurpy stories*. New York: Penguin.

Mack, J. (2013). *AH HA!* San Francisco, CA: Chronicle.

MacLachlan, P. (2013). *Snowflakes fall*. New York: Random House.

Morris, R. T. (2014). *This is a moose*. New York: Little, Brown.

Portis, A. (2014). *Froodle*. New York: Roaring Brook.

Scillian, D. (2013). *Memoirs of a hamster*. Ann Arbor, MI: Sleeping Bear.

Scillian, D. (2010). *Memoirs of a goldfish*. Ann Arbor, MI: Sleeping Bear.

Swenson, J. A. (2014). *If you were a dog*. New York: Farrar, Straus, Giroux.

Taylor, S. (2014). *Goal!* New York: Holt.

Viau, N. (2013). *Storm song*. Las Vegas, NV: Amazon.

CHAPTER 5: TEACHING ROUTINES

Aston, D. H. (2011). *A butterfly is patient*. San Francisco: Chronicle.

Banks, K. (2013). *City cat*. New York: Farrar Straus

Bishop, N. (2007). *Spiders.* New York: Scholastic.

Byrne, R. (2014). *This book just ate my dog!* New York: Holt.

Carney, E. (2009). *Frogs!* Washington, D. C.: National Geographic.

Cleary, B. P. (2015). *Ode to a commode: Concrete poems.* Minneapolis, MN: Millbrook.

Donaldson, J. (2010). *What the ladybug heard.* New York: Holt.

Donaldson, J. (2012). *Superworm.* New York: Scholastic.

Gibbons, G. (2012). *Ladybugs.* New York: Holiday House.

Graves, K. (2010). *Chicken Big.* San Francisco, CA: Chronicle.

Hamburg, J. (2013). *A mouse that says moo.* New York: Farrar Straus

Kasza, K. (2007). *Badger's fancy meal.* New York: Putnam.

Kosara, T. (2011). *Hibernation.* New York: Scholastic.

Krosoczka, J. J. (2014). *Peanut Butter and Jellyfish.* New York: Knopf.

Laminack, L. (2004). *Saturdays and teacakes.* Atlanta, GA: Peachtree.

LaRochelle, D. (2012). *It's a tiger!* San Francisco: Chronicle.

Lewis, J. P., & Florian, D. (2014). *Poem-mobiles: Crazy car poems.* New York: Schwartz & Wade.

Markle, S. (2011). *Butterfly tree.* Atlanta, GA: Peachtree.

Marsh, L. (2012). *Tigers.* Washington, D. C.: National Geographic.

Monks, L. (2004). *Aaaarrgghh! Spider!* Boston: Houghton Mifflin.

Pfeffer, W. (2004). *Wiggling worms at work.* New York: HarperCollins.

Rocco, J. (2013). *Super hair-o and the barber of doom.* New York: Hyperion.

Rosenthal, A. K. (2013). *Exclamation mark.* New York: Scholastic.

Seeger, L. V. (2013). *Bully.* New York: Roaring Brook.

Sheehan, K. (2014). *The Dandelion's Tale.* New York: Schwartz & Wade.

Sheth, K. (2013). *Tiger in my soup.* Atlanta, GA: Peachtree.

Sklansky, A. E. (2005). *Where do chicks come from?* New York: HarperCollins.

Thomson, B. (2013). *Fossil.* Las Vegas, NV: Amazon.

VanDerwater, A. L. (2013). *Forest has a song: Poems.* New York: Houghton Mifflin.

Willems, M. (2013). *I'm a frog!* New York: Hyperion.

Wilson, K. (2002). *Bear snores on.* New York: Simon & Schuster.

CHAPTER 6: INQUIRY EXPERIENCES—READING IN FOCUS

Allen, J. (2004). *Are you a bee?* Boston: Houghton Mifflin.

Aston, D. H. (2007). *A seed is sleepy.* San Francisco: Chronicle.

Bardhan-Quallen, S. (2014). *Duck, duck, moose!* New York: Hyperion.

Becker, A. (2013). *Journey.* Somerville, MA: Candlewick.

Bishop, N. (2012). *Snakes.* New York: Scholastic.

Boelts, M. (2007). *Those shoes.* Cambridge, MA: Candlewick.

Branley, F. (2002). *The sun our nearest star.* New York: HarperCollins.

Casanova, M. (2013). *One-dog sleigh.* New York: Farrar Straus.

Cecil, R. (2012). *Horsefly and Honeybee.* New York: Holt.

Cowcher, H. (2011). *Desert elephants.* New York: Farrar, Straus, Giroux.

Daly, C. (2014). *Emily's blue period.* New York: Roaring Brook.

Deacon, A. (2013). *Cheese belongs to you.* Somerville, MA: Candlewick.

dePaola, T. (1975). *Strega Nona.* New York: Simon & Schuster.

dePaola, T. (2002). *Adelita: A Mexican Cinderella story.* New York: Putnam.

Dudley, R. (2013). *Hank finds an egg.* White Plains, NY: Peter Pauper.

Emberley, R. (2009). *Chicken Little.* New York: Roaring Brook.

Emmett, J. (2011). *The princess and the pig*. New York: Walker.

Formento, A. (2012). *These bees count*. Chicago: Albert Whitman.

Fox, M. (1994). *Tough Boris*. Orlando, FL: Harcourt.

Galdone, P. (1973/2001). *The three billy goats gruff*. New York: Houghton Mifflin.

Galdone, P. (1975). *The gingerbread boy*. New York: Houghton Mifflin.

Geeslin, C. (2004). *Elena's Serenade*. New York: Atheneum.

Gibbons, G. (1983). *Sun up, sun down*. Orlando, FL: Harcourt.

Hong, L. T. (1993). *Two of everything*. Morton Grove, IL: Albert Whitman.

Hopkins, J. M. (2013). *Prairie Chicken Little*. Atlanta, GA: Peachtree.

Jordan, H. J. (1992). *How a seed grows*. New York: HarperCollins.

Kellogg, S. (1979). *Pinkerton, behave!* New York: Dial.

Kellogg, S. (1991). *Jack and the beanstalk*. New York: William Morrow.

Ketteman, H. (2012). *Señorita Gordita*. Chicago: Albert Whitman.

Kroll, S. (2001). *Patches lost and found*. Delray Beach, FL: Winslow Press.

Littledale, F. (1966). *The magic fish*. New York: Scholastic.

Louie, A. (1982). *Yen-Shen: A Cinderella story from China*. New York: Philomel.

Mahy, M. (1990). *The seven Chinese brothers*. New York: Scholastic.

Marino, G. (2012). *Too tall houses*. New York: Viking.

Marshall, J. (1987). *Red Riding Hood*. New York: Penguin.

Marshall, J. (1989). *Cinderella*. New York: Dial.

Marshall, J. (1989). *The Three Little Pigs*. New York: Dial.

Marshall, J. (1990). *Hansel and Gretel*. New York: Penguin.

Martin, R. (1992). *Rough-face girl*. Putnam.

Neubecker, R. (2013). *Winter is for snow*. New York: Hyperion.

Nolan, D. (2011). *Sea of dreams*. New York: Roaring Brook.

Pritchett, A. (2013). *Stick!* Somerville, MA: Candlewick.

Reid, B. (2013). *Picture a tree*. Chicago, IL: Albert Whitman.

Reynolds, A. (2012). *Creepy carrots*. New York: Simon & Schuster.

Reynolds, P. H. & Reynolds, P. A. (2014). *Going places*. New York: Atheneum.

Rosenthal, A. K. (2013). *Exclamation mark*. New York: Scholastic.

San Souci, R. D. (1989). *The talking eggs*. New York: Dial.

Steptoe, J. (1987). *Mufaro's beautiful daughters*. New York: William Morrow.

Sullivan, M. (2013). *Ball*. Boston: Houghton Mifflin.

Timmers, L. (2011). *Bang*. Minneapolis, MN: Lerner.

Wiesner, D. (2010). *Art & Max*. New York: Clarion.

Wiesner, D. (2013). *Mr. Wuffles*. New York: Clarion.

Willey, M. (2001). *Clever Beatrice*. New York: Simon & Schuster.

Woodson, J. (2012). *Each kindness*. New York: Penguin.

CHAPTER 7: INQUIRY EXPERIENCES—WRITING IN FOCUS

Aillaud, C. L. (2005). *Recess at 20 below*. Portland, OR: Graphic Arts Center.

Black, M. I. (2009). *Chicken cheeks*. New York: Simon & Schuster.

Briggs, R. (1978). *The snowman*. New York: Random House.

Browne, A. (1989) *Things I like*. New York: Random House.

Carle, E. (2000). *Does a kangaroo have a mother, too?* New York: HarperCollins.

Carle, E. (2014). *What's your favorite animal?* New York: Holt.

Charlip, R. (1964). *Fortunately.* New York: Aladdin/Simon & Schuster.

Demas, C. (2009). *Always in trouble.* New York: Scholastic

Diesen, D. (2013). *Picture day perfection.* New York: Abrams.

DiPucchio, K. (2014). *Dog days of school.* New York: Hyperion.

Emberley, R., Emberley, A., & Emberley, E. (2009). *There was an old monster!* New York: Orchard.

Evans, S. W. (2012). *We march.* New York: Roaring Brook.

Fleming, D. (2007). *Beetle bop.* Orlando, FL: Harcourt.

Fox, M. (2004). *Where is the green sheep?* Orlando, FL: Harcourt.

Frazier, C. (2010). *Lots of dots.* San Francisco, CA: Chronicle.

Gerber, C. (2013). *Seeds, bees, butterflies, and more! Poems for two voices.* New York: Holt.

Guiberson, B. Z. (2013). *The greatest dinosaur ever.* New York: Holt.

Hall, M. (2011). *Perfect square.* New York: HarperCollins.

Himmelman, J. (2010). *Pigs to the rescue.* New York: Holt.

Jenkins, S., & Page, R. (2003). *What do you do with a tail like this?* New York: Houghton Mifflin.

Jenkins, S., & Page, R. (2006). *Move!* New York: Houghton Mifflin.

Johnson, A. (2005). *A sweet smell of roses.* New York: Simon & Schuster.

Keane, D. (2009). *Sloppy Joe.* New York: HarperCollins.

Laminack, L. (2004). *Saturdays and teacakes.* Atlanta, GA: Peachtree.

Lewis, J. P. (2013). *Face bug.* Honesdale, PA: Wordsong.

Long, E. (2011). *The book that Zack wrote.* Maplewood, NJ: Blue Apple Books.

Mack, J. (2012). *Good news, bad news.* San Francisco, CA: Chronicle.

McDonnell, P. (2011). *Me . . . Jane.* New York: Little, Brown.

McGinty, A. B. (2013). *Gandhi: A march to the sea.* Las Vegas, NV: Amazon.

Meltzer, B. (2014). *I am Abraham Lincoln.* New York: Dial.

Morstad, J. (2013). *How to.* Canada: Simply Read Books.

Muth, J. J. (2014). *Hi, Koo! A year of seasons.* New York: Scholastic.

O'Connor, J. (2008). *Fancy Nancy: Bonjour, butterfly.* New York: HarperCollins.

Offill, J. (2014). *Sparky!* New York: Schwartz & Wade.

Pearson, S. (2011). *How to teach a slug to read.* Tarrytown, NY: Marshall Cavendish.

Robinson, M. (2013). *How to wash a woolly mammoth.* New York: Holt.

Rohmann, E. (2002). *My friend Rabbit.* New York: Square Fish.

Rosenthal, A. K. (2009). *Yes day!* New York: HarperCollins.

Seeger, L. V. (2007). *First the egg.* New Milford, CT: Roaring Brook.

Seuss, D. (1971). *The Lorax.* New York: Random House.

Singer, M. (2013). *Follow, follow.* New York: Dial.

Stone, T. L. (2013). *Who says women can't be doctors? The story of Elizabeth Blackwell.* New York: Holt.

Taylor, S. (2006). *When a monster is born.* New York: Roaring Brook.

Viorst, J. (2010). *Lulu and the brontosaurus.* New York: Atheneum.

Waber, B. (1972/2000). *Ira sleeps over.* New York: Houghton Mifflin.

Weatherford, C. B. (2005). *Freedom on the menu: The Greensboro sit-ins.* New York: Dial.

Winter, J. (2011). *The watcher: Jane Goodall's life with the chimps.* New York: Schwartz & Wade.

Online Resources

Go to teacherexpress.scholastic.com/transforming-literacy-teaching-K-2 to download or view the following free resources.

Downloadable Print Resources

- Kindergarten Foundational Skills and Language Standards Planning Guide
- Grade 1 Foundational Skills and Language Standards Planning Guide
- Grade 2 Foundational Skills and Language Standards Planning Guide
- Kindergarten Reading Standards Planning Guide
- Grade 1 Reading Standards Planning Guide
- Grade 2 Reading Standards Planning Guide
- Be an Observer Notebook
- Sample Anecdotal Note Sheet for Writing Workshop
- Brain Map
- Comprehension Conversations Parent Notes
- Five-Finger Retell
- Character Trait Web
- Character Reaction Chart
- Character Decision Chart
- Character Transformation Chart
- Comparing Cinderella Versions Chart
- Little Books Self-Evaluation
- Poetry Paper

Video Resources

- Classroom Tour
- Standards Integration in Action
- Reading Workshop in Action
- Writing Workshop in Action
- Teaching Routines in Action
- Inquiry Experiences—Reading in Action
- Inquiry Experiences—Writing in Action

Transforming Literacy Teaching in the Era of Higher Standards, K–2 © 2015 by Maria P. Walther, Scholastic Teaching Resources